Unseen People

"In the fascinating pages of *Unseen People,* you will get to journey with a true global ambassador of hope, DeAnna Sanders. I have had the privilege of seeing some of DeAnna's love, warmth, humor, and hope shine in all kinds of places, for all kinds of people: from Oklahoma to Georgia to Indonesia. She doesn't serve up a wistful kind of hope. Rather, she offers the kind that creates change in people across the street and around the world. Enjoy big helpings for yourself and watch the people you touch light up."

—Michele Rickett
Founder and CEO
She Is Safe

"DeAnna has long used the written word to share her heart for the lost and the mission believers have to share the love of God. *Unseen People* brings this vital message together to help open more eyes to the hope of Christ."

—Reagan Jackson
Managing Editor for Adult Resources
National Woman's Missionary Union, Birmingham, AL

"DeAnna weaves together the stories of her life in an engaging and entertaining way as she points to the hand of God, Who guided her to be on mission in every stage and season of life. *Unseen People* will challenge you to see the world with God's eyes and join in His great work where you are."

—Dr. Bryan Pain
Senior Pastor
First Baptist Duncan

"DeAnna Sanders has always had a gift for storytelling and love for missions. Through *Unseen People,* DeAnna reflects on life lessons from ministering abroad to sipping coffee in the quietness of her own home. She informs us through her experiences, inspires us through her words, and challenges us through her direct questions to the reader. I encourage you to read, reflect, and respond whether you choose to read this book in a week or an essay at time for your daily devotion. You will be blessed by her words."

—Deborah Root, Ed.D.
Professor and Chair of Communications
Ouachita Baptist University

"DeAnna invites us to her back porch and around the world, challenging us to see, hear, and really notice God at work in all He has created."

—Danette High
Emeritus Missionary
International Mission Board

"Reflective, spiritual, personal, absorbing, and always authentic, DeAnna Sander's *Unseen People* challenges us all to live boldly and to push through whatever fears keep us from seeing the humanity and uniqueness of the people around us. While DeAnna has traveled the world in her missionary work, we can all lead lives of blessed purpose, whether in Kathmandu or in our own neighborhoods."

—Susan Madon, CFRE, CEO
Minerva Nonprofit Management Consulting

"DeAnna takes us on a journey around the world and opens our eyes to see the unseen—people and places. As she shares her life story, she even challenges us to ask ourselves who we are, and how we would like to be seen and known. DeAnna's heartwarming stories remind us that God is everywhere, and He is always working. And she provokes us to see the unseen people in our own lives through God's eyes."

—Arlene Johnson
VP of Donor Development
Trinity Broadcast Network

Sharing Light and Life with Your
Neighbors and the Nations

Unseen People

DeAnna Lynn Sanders

AMBASSADOR INTERNATIONAL
GREENVILLE, SOUTH CAROLINA & BELFAST, NORTHERN IRELAND

www.ambassador-international.com

Unseen People
Sharing Light and Life with Your Neighbors and the Nations
©2024 by DeAnna Lynn Sanders
All rights reserved

ISBN: 978-1-64960-541-2, hardcover
ISBN: 978-1-64960-508-5, paperback
eISBN: 978-1-64960-551-1
Library of Congress Control Number: 2024940482

Cover Design by Hannah Linder Designs
Interior Typesetting by Dentelle Design

No part of this publication may be reproduced, distributed, or transmitted in any form or by any means, including photocopying, recording, or other electronic or mechanical methods, without the prior written permission of the publisher, except in the case of brief quotations embodied in critical reviews and certain other noncommercial uses permitted by copyright law. For permission requests, contact the publisher using the information below.

All Scriptural quotations are taken from The Holy Bible, English Standard Version (ESV), Copyright 2001 by Crossway, a publishing ministry of Good News Publishers. All rights reserved. ESV Text Edition: 2011.

Ambassador International titles may be purchased in bulk for education, business, fundraising, or sales promotional use. For information, please email sales@emeraldhouse.com.

AMBASSADOR INTERNATIONAL	AMBASSADOR BOOKS
Emerald House	The Mount
411 University Ridge, Suite B14	2 Woodstock Link
Greenville, SC 29601	Belfast, BT6 8DD
United States	Northern Ireland, United Kingdom
www.ambassador-international.com	www.ambassadormedia.co.uk

The colophon is a trademark of Ambassador, a Christian publishing company.

To my husband, Johnny, who has supported my journeys into all the world.

Forty years ago, we said to each other, "I pledge my life to you in the love of Jesus Christ our Lord." Since that day, you willingly gave me freedom to go and serve and to stay home and write. Together, we have given to the world our amazing, beautiful children and grandchildren.

And to my parents, Don and Johnette Travis, who are both with Jesus now.

They laid a rich foundation of strong faith and unconditional love for our family and others. They demonstrated daily what it looked like to love each other, next-door neighbors, and the unseen people of all nations.

Table of Contents

Foreword 1

Acknowledgments 3

Introduction 5

1
Learning to See the Unseen 11

2
Seeing the Unseen from My Minivan 29

3
Seeing and Listening to Unseen People 41

4
Seeing People Virtually 53

5
Seeing and Meeting Unseen People in My Neighborhood 73

6
Seeing the Underserved in a Nation of Plenty 87

7
Learning from Unseen People in Planes, Trains, and Automobiles 105

8
Looking the Unseen in the Eyes 123

9
Listen to Unheard Women 135

10
Unseen Precious Children 139

11
A Dog's Perspective on Seeing the Unseen 145

12
Sharing the Stories of Unseen People 155

Conclusion 161
Travel Map 165
Bibliography 167
About the Author 169

> "What does love look like?
> It has the hands to help others. It has the feet to hasten to the poor and needy. It has eyes to see misery and want. It has the ears to hear the sighs and sorrows of men."
>
> —Augustine of Hippo, *The Confessions*

Foreword

IN MY SIXTEEN YEARS WITH She Is Safe, an international anti-trafficking nonprofit, I've interacted with thousands of women and girls around the globe. Many of their stories are hard—they are facing atrocities too horrible to even dare to imagine. When we see the sheer realities, it is easy to be overwhelmed or to become numb. But Jesus gives us the invitation to lean in. It can be uncomfortable to really see people—their pain, their loves, their passions and their transformation. Yet each one is a gift of God, created by Him and for Him; and that reflects Him and His goodness in a special way. It is when we lean in that we are close enough to share light and life and also have the opportunity to learn and to be changed ourselves.

I met DeAnna Sanders in the San Francisco airport on our way to Indonesia in 2011. She had recently joined the staff of She Is Safe to help take on the leadership of our work in Indonesia. Among other things on that trip, she was plunged into the firehose of five days of me teaching lots of math—not her favorite. Yet she navigated that experience and her new role with grace and wisdom. For more than a decade, I've watched DeAnna push through her own comfort zones in order to see, serve, and learn from people in her community and around the globe. Along the way, DeAnna has become a cherished friend.

Through *Unseen People: Sharing Light and Life with Your Neighbors and the Nations,* you will be enriched by DeAnna's lifetime of experience. She uses short, engaging anecdotes to transport you from her back porch to the local hospital and communities around the globe, giving you eyes to see and experience people from different cultures without ever hopping on a plane.

While I've dedicated my life to seeing and serving people from the hardest places, in these pages, I was also challenged to think through and notice those whom I often don't really see right here around me. As you read this book, I encourage you to ask God these simple questions: God, who do you want me to see today? And how do you want me to respond?

Katy Anderson, ThM
Vice President, International
She Is Safe

Acknowledgments

WHERE WOULD I BE WITHOUT Jesus? I would be unseen, unknown, and unloved. Thank You, Lord, for all good gifts, especially for blessing me with Your salvation and for the words to write and share.

If it were not for you, dear readers, these words would be seen only by God and me. Thank you for reading, encouraging, and sharing with others words you have received from me through the years.

My love language is encouragement. My brother and sister, Donny and Debbie, I am grateful that you speak my language by encouraging me in so many ways. And to my Sanders family, especially my mother-in-law, thank you for helping me to come and go, to be on mission from the Oklahoma Panhandle to the Indonesian islands, caring for my family tenderly through all those years.

Thank you to the many who have fanned the flame within me to write, edit, and write again, including my communications professor at Ouachita Baptist University, Dr. Downs, who encouraged me with his red editing pen to make my words stronger.

My first regular publishing gig was with Woman's Missionary Union who gave me ample opportunity to combine my love for writing with igniting a life-long mission passion in teenage girls through writing curriculum. Thank you, editors, for that opportunity and for other assignments through the years.

Thank you to the people of Immanuel Baptist Church in Duncan, Oklahoma, who allowed me to be your minister of missions for almost ten years. You gave me opportunity to lead us to love the people of our community and also to learn how to go into all the world and take you with me.

To the staff at She Is Safe, you led me to fall in love with the sweet people of Indonesia. They remain forever in my heart. Your vision to prevent, rescue, and restore women and girls from slavery and abuse is such a noble purpose. Thank you for letting me share it.

First Baptist Church in Duncan, Oklahoma, you are my faith family that I cannot imagine doing life without week after week. Thank you for opportunities to serve, worship, and grow as a disciple.

Ambassador International, thank you for taking a chance on a seasoned writer but an unpublished author. You do such good God-ordained work of promoting the Gospel through the written word. I am so glad you have helped me and so many others artfully share our message with a waiting world. Thank you for what you do.

Introduction

IF YOU WERE INTRODUCING YOURSELF to a new person, how would you describe yourself? I would say that I am first, an introvert. (I love my home and get my energy from solitude.) After we chatted for a few minutes, we would learn more about each other. You would learn that I am also a writer of blogs, newsletters, and sometimes social media. I love to help faith-based nonprofits because I worked for one—She Is Safe—for almost ten years, helping women and girls escape and recover from human trafficking and abuse. I have been around the world multiple times to mostly unseen locations to hear the stories of unseen people. That is what I do now. I am a storyteller.

I am also a coffee snob. I love good coffee, usually black; but sometimes, I will drink a skinny latte—or even better, a cold brew skinny latte. I am a dog-lover, a birdwatcher, a walker, and a lover of books. Most importantly, you would learn that I am a follower of Jesus.

You may not learn all of that from me in the first conversation. It takes time to get to know a person. You start with a name, a smile, and a listening ear. Those are actions you may do naturally, but some of us need a few reminders. It does not matter where you are—city, suburbs, small town, or on a rural route—I encourage you to call people by their names. Who knows? That one small step could be the beginning, the first layer of a friendship, an opportunity to share the love of Christ with them. You do not have to feel like you need to change the world today. Just learn someone's name.

Our name sets us apart. When someone says our name out loud, we feel seen. And we are reminded that God saw us first. "But now thus says the Lord, he who created you, O Jacob, he who formed you, O Israel: 'Fear not, for I have redeemed you; I have called you by name, you are mine'" (Isa. 43:1).

Of course, God values our entire being, not just our names. Sadly, many people do not know that they are priceless. We are all seen, treasured, and loved. That is who we are. You could even use those three words as your identifying descriptors.

To understand the depth of God's great love for us, read Psalm 139:1-18. Take time to read it now, slowly. Let the wonder of it sink in. What did you discover? The Scripture says He knows us intimately, fully. He is always with us. Tragically, people do not know they are seen and loved by God. It starts with you showing them that love. For you to see them, you need to say their name.

I love stories in Scripture where God sees people. Do you remember the story of Sarah's servant, Hagar, in Genesis 16? Hagar proclaims in that dramatic encounter with God that He is *the God Who Sees*. Throughout the Gospels, we have stories describing how Jesus sees women in the midst of their pain—as in the story of Mary Magdalene, the woman caught in adultery, the bleeding woman, and so many others. Take time soon to spend time in Scripture to see how often God the Father and God the Son call previously unseen people by their names and in the midst of their troubles.

Who are the people in your neighborhood, at your kid's school, or at your workplace who need to be seen, heard, and shown God's love? Do you know the name of the cashier at your local supermarket? Accept the challenge to see them, know them, and call them by name. God calls us to see people starting in our homes, in our neighborhoods, and onward to the nations.

My parents instilled in me a love for all people of the world—from my daddy as he preached about the Great Commission and from Mama as she shared about missionaries around the world in her women's group that often met in our home. I first felt a call to missions as a freshman at Ouachita Baptist University. God placed in me the desire to go into all the world and also to write. When I said yes to God's call, I did not know it would involve being in a small boat in a big ocean speeding around the islands of Indonesia off the coast of Sumatra.

I actually like to be near water. Who does not like the smell of sea salt and the rhythmic sound of the ocean waves licking the shore? I just do not want to be immersed in the water. I like to think I have enough swimming skills that I could save myself if the alternative was death by drowning. But I am not sure I could and have no desire to test my theory. So when I found myself in uncharted waters gripping a small lifejacket, I would ask myself, *Why did I want to go here?*

People often ask me that question about my travels. For many years, I was either prepping for a trip, returning from a trip, or planning another one. In the past thirty years, it has meant going to places like Central Mexico, Bolivia, South Africa, Bangladesh, India, and Indonesia. I can see the question forming in their eyes. Sometimes, they even say out loud, "Why do you want to go there?"

I know what they are asking. If you save all that money for travel, why would you not like to go somewhere fun? Except for trips that had a mission focus but were still notable travel destinations like Rome and London, most people just do not understand why I would go to challenging, unheard-of places. But I did want to go there. I wanted to meet the people. I wanted to hear their stories, to understand their culture. I wanted to visit them in their homes, sit on their floors, and drink their strong coffee. It was all fascinating to me.

I have had several family members say to me, "It scares me when you travel to [insert a destination listed above]. I am always glad to hear when you've made it back home safely." And they will ask, "Don't you feel scared? Are you ever in danger?" Yes, I am. Is it easy travel? No, it is not. Am I pushed beyond my limits? I absolutely am, every time. But it is what I am supposed to do. It is where I am supposed to be.

In fact, I have struggled more with staying home. My comfortable life is very . . . well, it is warm and cozy. I say that now as I write from my cushy chair with my fancy laptop. I am nice and comfy—not that comfort is bad. But sometimes, when I am enjoying my life, I think about the throngs of people pressing in all around our car in sweltering Dhaka, Bangladesh. I think about the mothers on one of the small, obscure outer islands in Indonesia. Very few people even know they are there or that their island exists. I think about the tribe in South Africa that is a mixture of races. They are even rejected by people in their own country. I wanted to go to let them know they were seen and that they mattered and to show them God's love through the ministry of presence.

The same people who question my going halfway around the world and back again are the same people who say, "But people here need to know about Jesus, too." And I say, "Yes, absolutely. Are you telling them?" What I want to say is, "You stay here and do that, and I will happily pack my bags and go to the other side of the world."

It was harder for me to see the needs of lonely people in the grocery store near my home, or my neighbors right next door living lives of loneliness and despair, or homeless people wandering the streets in my own small Oklahoma town. I have learned that being on mission is just geography. The needs of people know no boundaries. One is no more important than the other. The need is both-and, not either-or.

So, why did I go to those places? Why did I go from my neighborhood to the nations? Why do you want to go? Are you ready?

Those are all good questions. This is my journey and my attempt to answer those concerns and encourage you to go prepared to the difficult places, whether that is nearby or across the ocean (or in the ocean).

This is my voyage into the unknown—from next door to the nations. These bite-sized snippets from my life are not necessarily in chronological order. Some of the stories overlap, but they all show through my family, work, church, and travel experiences that God continued to help me focus my vision on the unseen. As we weave through the stories together, we will sip lattes on my deck while the cardinals chirp and hummingbirds buzz overhead. You are invited to walk with me next door and meet my neighbors or wonder who is behind the door in the third house on the left down the street. Join me in the small boat on a big ocean off the shores of Indonesia. Thanks for joining me. But be warned—it is not always comfortable to see what has been hidden in plain sight from your view. Corrected vision promises both pain and beauty to unfocused eyes. Trust me. The view is worth the wait.

1
Learning to See the Unseen

I LEARNED THROUGH EXPERIENCE THAT God has an interesting sense of humor. I knew at one point that He wanted me to take seriously His command to "'Go therefore and make disciples of all nations'" (Matt. 28:19) and tell all the people about Him. But the thing is, I did not even want to be around people. Truth is, I did not even like them very much. But I am getting ahead of myself.

It was 1966. I was six years old, living in Reid, Alabama, a sparsely populated, rural community. I remember going places with my daddy, who was the pastor of the Baptist church in that northern Alabama community. Wherever we went, it seemed it was either to the church or visiting with people. Sometimes, those people were church members who just wanted to chat. Sometimes, they were people who were mourning the loss of a child in a car accident. All I remember was that Daddy was a listener and that people seemed to be calmer around him and wanted him there in the chaos of life. I remember going places with my daddy and seeing him do what he did best, minister to people. I saw him see so many people others overlooked.

I remember going on mission trips with Daddy. We took teenagers from south Arkansas to Flint, Michigan; Pittsburg, Pennsylvania; and Washington, D.C. Those were trips that etched vivid memories. They opened the eyes of kids who had never traveled outside their state to see the needs of people who were very different from themselves. I remember hot, bumpy rides in our church bus, which was a white-painted version of an old yellow school bus.

On one of those trips, I was trying to give Daddy driving directions as we entered the D.C. suburbs. I had spent the previous summer in the area as a short-term missionary. I do not think it qualified me on giving directions on the Beltway. But there I was, sitting behind him as he drove and giving very specific directions such as, "Turn that way . . . no . . . that way . . . I mean. . . ." I got us very lost. Even though he was frustrated, Daddy was patient and eventually got us to our destination. I thought I was the expert on D.C. since I had spent a summer there, but Daddy was always the one who seemed to get me out of situations when I was challenged—directionally and otherwise.

I went to many places with Daddy when I was growing up. He was always excited to hear about places where my ministries took me as an adult—Mexico, London, Bangladesh, and Indonesia. Since I felt like Daddy instilled in me the desire to go where God called, I felt like he was okay that I was working in one of those places when he died.

One of the last places I went with Daddy was to the hospital following his brain surgery. I do not think he knew I was there, and I choose not to remember him that way. I would rather remember him when people would call him Brother Don or Reverend Don, and I would be happy that I could just call him Daddy.

In one of the small communities where he served, I recall my first memories of Easter in Mount Ida, Arkansas, when I was five years old. I do not remember the details of the community Easter egg hunt, except that I was there and I was eager to find as many eggs as I could, especially the prize golden egg. When you found that, it meant you were special and maybe not so little anymore.

I had my basket, and I awaited the signal. It was going to be a good day. I could feel it. "GO!" someone yelled; and off I went as fast as my kindergarten legs would go, scooping up eggs along the way. Kids were everywhere, squealing and scattering throughout the playground in search of brightly colored eggs.

Then, I saw it—the golden egg—the treasure everyone was seeking. And it was mine, all mine! Everyone was still searching for it, and it was already in my basket!

I do not remember any other details other than how it made me feel, and I wanted to keep it and treasure it and not share it with anyone. So that is what I did. I took it home and hid it where no one could find it. It lay deep within my toy box, along with my many other priceless treasures, including my stuffed monkey, Bim, and my toy pop gun.

All was well with my world until a few days later. My mother came in to clean my bedroom. She smelled something pungent and awful. I knew what it was.

"DeAnna Lynn," she said using both my first and middle names, which meant I was definitely in trouble. "What is that smell?" I dug into my toy box and reluctantly revealed the culprit—my beautiful golden prize egg. I showed it to my mama, and she smiled and told me she was sorry but that we had to throw it away. That was the end of that.

I do not remember learning any life lessons at that moment in time. I was just so sad that I no longer got to keep the one thing that made me feel so great a few days earlier. I had placed such value in a disposable treasure. That little five-year-old preacher's kid would learn through the years the wisdom of Matthew 6:21: "'For where your treasure is, there your heart will be also.'" So, let your treasure be not an earthly thing but one that lasts forever, the things only of God. I would also learn the Scripture from Luke 2:19 about Jesus' mother observing her Son teaching in the temple as a Boy. "But Mary treasured up all these things, pondering them in her heart."

Lesson learned: keep the treasure in your heart; do not store it in your toy chest. The odor will surely reveal your stinky heart.

The Girl Who Didn't Like to Talk

Once upon a time, there was a little girl. When people thought of her, they did not remember her voice but recalled that she sat comfortably in a quiet corner of the room, content with a book to read and a snack to eat. She was a nice girl but did not have too much to say. The proverbial wallflower was easy to overlook and remain unseen.

That little girl grew up and decided to put her thoughts not into spoken words but into written words. She loved to read. She loved to write. And she loved all peoples in all cultures of the world. She decided to make that her life's calling—a writer to the world, traveling to the nations to gather stories and make unknown people known and unseen people seen. It was a good calling and something she could do until she learned that her college major, Mass Communications, required her to not only complete writing courses but also to take speech classes.

That is when it began. The sheer terror of speaking to a group of people was overwhelming. She did not want everyone looking as she said the words she had carefully researched and constructed. Why could she not just make copies of her speech, and they could read her words? That is not how it works in college classrooms. That is not how it works when church congregations want to hear a verbal report from the girl about her adventures in summer missions in Washington, D.C. Somehow, she made it through four years of speech classes and other presentations, even though nausea was a constant threat every time a podium and a microphone awaited. She was shy, soft-spoken, and very afraid.

That was me for most of my life—the girl who did not like to talk, especially not in public. I had heard that at one time, the fear of public speaking was the number one fear of American adults. That was me until my fear of being in a small boat on the open sea took over as my number one fear. I will tell you more about that later.

What is it about speaking in front of other people that is utterly terrifying to many of us? You could say it would be the fear of saying something stupid and making a fool of yourself in front of strangers. It could be the fear of forgetting everything you wanted to say and standing there like an absolute idiot for all the world to see. Probably, the bottom line is insecurity in who you are as a person and feeling like what you have to say is unimportant. We have low self esteem and are insecure and quiet.

Of course, being an introvert is an issue when it comes to public speaking. I used to think being an introvert meant I did not like people. I knew that was not true. I find people fascinating and cultures so very interesting. It was an epiphany for me when I learned just a few years ago that introverts do like people. It is just that people zap their energy, and introverts need quiet space to recharge. That is me. Extroverts also like people and enjoy the energy they receive from other people. It keeps their engines running. That is Johnny, my husband. I know that when I am traveling or when I am required to make public appearances or any event that requires me to be around a group of people for very long, I will require some time following those events that include long, quiet times alone. It is such a good thing to know that I actually do like people!

Today, the girl who did not like to talk finds herself frequently speaking to groups: a room filled with college students, a small group of church women, a room full of community leaders and professionals, and sometimes, even to a television camera. Very often, when I traveled to Indonesia, I was asked when I returned to say something encouraging to a church group or other gathering of people. That is all very stressful for a girl who would rather be typing than speaking.

What I have found is God wants to shine through me. He wants to speak words of encouragement and challenge through me, so He equips me to do so. He gives me frequent opportunities to be His mouthpiece. He invites me to ask others to be involved in this process as they pray for me to get through these public speaking challenges.

Do you know what else I have found? The very real passion that I feel for the work I have done takes over. When I was telling stories of girls who were trapped in the terror of sex trafficking and abuse, I did not think about what others were thinking of me. I was thinking about how much I wanted people to understand the horrible conditions some women and girls have endured. I wanted people who were listening to understand that there were actions we needed to take to make a difference. I wanted people to see the unseen. I wanted people to hear the cries of the persecuted and lonely and those whose voices were muffled. I wanted them to hear the ones that would like to speak but were silenced because their basic human freedoms had been stolen. I got to be their mouthpiece. Somehow, the girl who did not like to talk could not wait to tell others' stories that needed to be heard. Do I still get nervous? I do. Yet God is still good and always equips those He calls.

I have read the plea of the apostle Paul, and I echo his heart when he wrote in Ephesians 6:18-20, "To that end, keep alert with all perseverance, making supplication for all the saints, and also for me, that words may be given to me in opening my mouth boldly to proclaim the mystery of the gospel, for which I am an ambassador in chains, that I may declare it boldly, as I ought to speak."

What Did You Want to Be When You Grew Up?

I asked that question to the adult Sunday school class I was teaching. It served as a lead-in question to spur our thinking about the Scripture in Ephesians 4 we focused on that morning. The follow-up question was, "With the career you now have, what are some personal characteristics required to help you do what you do?"

"I wanted to be an astronaut or the first female secretary of state," the now fifth-grade science teacher said with a smile. "My job teaching requires patience, vision, and love."

"I wanted to be a soldier, since my dad was in the military. And I followed in his footsteps. My work requires patience, endurance, and selflessness."

"I wanted to be a vet, since I loved animals so much. Then I realized you have to be good at math and science, and you have to operate on bloody animals." That was my answer. That one obviously did not work out. The life of a writer requires solitude, stability, and creativity.

Looking back, I can see how God weaved it all together. Soon after I dreamed about being a vet, I realized I had an artistic bent. I could draw, but I was a better writer. Countless notebooks full of scribbled words proved my love for the written word. Soon after that call on my life, I felt God leading me to serve others through international missions. Why not put those two passions together? I dreamed of traveling abroad to where missionaries served in foreign and exotic locations and capturing their lives through words and photos.

Then life happened. Marriage and babies came complete with mounds of laundry, making school lunches every morning, and cooking family dinners every night. After a few years, I found my words again. I began writing mission curriculum for teenage girls so they could understand the call of God on their lives as they went into all the world. About ten years later, God opened the door for me to be the missions minister at my church to mobilize members to be on mission. I had my passport stamped multiple times from Mexico to South Africa and England to Bangladesh. I learned about cross-cultural ministry, how to travel internationally, and how to serve among "the least of these." Along the way, I misplaced my words again.

The next door God opened was for me to go deeper into one country, Indonesia, for the nonprofit organization, She Is Safe. My words came back as I talked with women and girls and learned about their lives and their dreams and how they could realize them. I absorbed all those moments, sat on mats on their floors, took copious notes, and came home and wrote about those people and how they are changing and how they changed me.

Almost seven years later, another door opened at my organization. It was all printed on a business card: Global Communications Officer. Anytime I looked at those first two words, it made me think God had made my life into one grand loop, linking together my love for the people of the world and my desire to communicate the needs of women and girls and how we all can best help them to be safe and free. It required much solitude as I sat in my office in front of my laptop instead of spending many hours on airplanes on transcontinental flights. It required that I was okay with a stable life and not the hectic travel-planning and going and recovering to which I had become accustomed. It required creativity to see the world and to see the unseen through the eyes of a writer and not a traveler. It gave me more time to tell the stories of girls I had met who were born in brothels, of young women tricked into a life of prostitution, and of moms who were learning job skills so they could send their little girls to school. I told all those stories and new ones I heard from She Is Safe coworkers.

I looked at my new business card again—Global Communications Officer. I and all the animals of the world are thankful it did not say, "Global Veterinarian Officer."

Who's Around Your Table Today?

Whom did you invite to join you around your table today? Are they all family? Or did you invite someone others overlooked, someone unseen?

It was Thanksgiving, my favorite holiday—the day for families to be together and enjoy all the festive food. For my Southern family, that meant roasted turkey, cornbread dressing, green bean casserole, broccoli and rice casserole, green stuff (lime gelatin, fruit, and whipped topping), cranberry sauce, and, of course, pies. One of my favorites my grandmother made—and now my mother-in-law makes—was pecan pie. (Of course, my favorite is chocolate pie. Hopefully, that is on the Christmas dinner lineup—all great food for a diabetic like myself.)

Of course, the important part is not about the food, it is about the people around the table. The kitchen table in my home is often empty throughout the week. Now, on many Saturday evenings, our kids, their spouses, and our grandchildren join me and my husband and crowd around the kitchen table or the longer table on our deck when the weather is nice. We enjoy a feast featuring some type of grilled or smoked meat that Johnny has crafted for us.

As I think about my table and the people around it, I remember my childhood and the people my parents would invite to join us for dinner. Daddy was a sweet and gentle soul. When he sensed someone needed to be with a family, he invited them to ours. I am sure I do not remember them all, but I do remember a little girl, about six years old, who was not able to go to her home one night. I have no idea why. I was about seven at the time. I just remember that she was afraid. She was dirty. She smelled bad. And she was hungry. I do not even remember her name, but she came home with us and sat at our table for one night—and she was family.

Then there was Gino Martini. I always wondered if that was his real name. He was a high school exchange student who came to us from Lima, Peru. When he arrived, he graciously brought a gift—a bottle of wine. For most people, that would be a great gift. For a conservative teetotaler Baptist pastor in southwestern Tennessee, that gift was poured down the sink. We kept the decorative bottle tucked away in the cabinet as a reminder of our year with Gino. I wonder what happened to that guy when he went back to South America. All I know is he taught us a few words of Spanish. Even though he was Roman Catholic, he went with us to our church; and for a year, he sat around our table, and he was family.

One year, my cousin, Yvonne, was dealing with difficult teenage issues and needed another family to live with for a while. Daddy invited her to join us. I do not know if those problems got better; but for a few months, she laughed with us and shared our home and our table, and she was family.

I have learned that God weaves people in and out of our lives, and we are always enriched by their presence. Sometimes, we learn big things; and sometimes, we just need to share turkey, a hamburger, or pie and coffee and just be family together.

This is Me

I bought my husband, Johnny, a kit for determining his ancestry for his Father's Day gift. He loved it. He has had great fun tracing his roots and sharing his new information with his family. In fact, he loves sharing with anyone who will listen, family or not. There is a reason those kits are so popular. Everyone wants to know their origins. There is nothing wrong with that. We all want to know our roots. We all want to see people from our past and learn from them.

I was born the third child in a family with *D* names. My brother is Donny (until he grew up and decided to go by his given name, Don). My sister is Debbie (two *D*s, actually—Deborah Diane). And then there was me. My parents wondered what to name another girl with a *D*. My mother consulted her mother. One of Mawma Bradford's favorite actresses back in the day was Deanna Durbin. They chose DeAnna (given by one grandmother) and my middle name, Lynn (in honor of my other grandmother, Linnie). Mama had her way with the spelling of my name. Capital *A* so no one would call me Dianna. Sorry, Mama. It did not matter. I get called that very often, along with Deann, Dina, and Debbie. But that is okay. I like being unique. At least, I do now. Never being able to find my name on a keychain or necklace was frustrating growing up. I have learned to let that go. I am not bitter at all.

Deanna Durbin was born in Canada, became a Hollywood actress, and then lived in France. During my first visit to Indonesia, I learned that a popular song had been used with my name (spelled differently, of course).

Deanna is also a Hispanic name. They have a way of saying my name lyrically and not with a slow Southern drawl I am used to hearing. I love that my name has an international flair. When I went to Indonesia the first time, a sign was hung in the guestroom of our host's home that said, "Welcome Cherylann, Kathy, and Dean." They got Cherylann's name correct. Katy and DeAnna have giggled about that still many years later.

I know who I am. I am a most loved, treasured, daughter of the King. That is all that matters. He knows where I am and how to spell my name. He knows me. He sees me. I am grateful for that. Who are you? How would you like to be seen and known?

This Is Why I Am Here

I hear voices. I do not see dead people, but I do hear voices. Sometimes, it is a voice that makes me doubt who I am and what I do and makes me wonder why I am here. Maybe you hear those voices, too.

It makes me consider, why am I here on earth? Why did God make me and place me on this planet in this place in time? One would think that after sixty-plus years on this earth, I would not let these voices get into my head. But they do from time to time. To quieten them, I will offer a few answers.

When I was a child, my first memory of what I wanted to be went from being a veterinarian to an artist to a writer. As a seventeen-year-old, I heard another Voice that gently urged me to answer the call into a life of ministry and missions. I said yes. I knew that this was why I was here. Then I met Johnny. I found myself a wife and, soon after, a mother of two. Now a grandmother of five, I look into their sweet faces; and when I hear them say, "Hi, Bebe!" in their little voices as they run into my home, I know that this is what I am here for.

Eventually, the Voice that led me into ministry combined my roles, and I became a writer of missions curriculum for teenage girls. That path led me into a ten-year career, and I found fulfillment as I stayed home with my children and wrote. As I sat at my computer and helped girls discover the world, I knew that this was why I was here. And then the true Voice led me to help my church be on mission. I became a missions minister for almost ten years and helped many church members find their place in the world, whether it was in distributing food to those in need in our town or on one of many international mission locations. I knew this was why God put me on this earth.

But the Voice was not finished. As rewarding as my work with She Is Safe was, it was not without its challenges. In the years I served on staff with She Is Safe, both of my parents passed away. My daddy's death happened while I was in Indonesia; but by God's grace, I made it back in time for the funeral. Also during this time, my husband fell and broke a vertebra in his back that required surgery and months of recovery. During one trip, I was sick with stomach bugs and endured challenging team member situations. When I returned home, my house had been flooded due to a burst water line, which caused major damage and upheaval in our living situation. Upon returning from another trip, I discovered that my sweet dog, Daisy, had torn her ACL and required surgery. Three months later, she was still recovering.

Amid all those challenges, I heard that old voice of doubt nestled into my brain. It made me wonder whether I was doing the right thing. Maybe I should just stay home so I could attend to all these crises better. Surely, someone better equipped and younger could do this job. Why was I really doing this? I could find something easier to do with my life. Those thoughts made me pause and address the voice of discouragement. I let that voice know that I would do the work God called me to do until He said to stop and move on. My job was to listen to that Voice and obey.

So, what is the answer? Why am I here? Is it to be a writer? Is it to be a missions leader? Should I be a wife, mother, and grandmother? What about being an advocate for abused and exploited women and girls?

The answer is yes to all of the above. Ultimately, I am here on this earth to know God (the Voice) and to make Him known through my verbal and written words, through my travels throughout the world, through nurturing my family, and through my listening to stories of Indonesian women and girls and telling them to you. I am here to see the unseen.

The Best Sugar Stop of All

The waiting room of a hospital is an interesting place to people-watch. It is a place to see so many people dealing with their unseen medical challenges. It is also amazing the valuable information you can learn while sitting in a hospital waiting room. When is it seasonally acceptable to go barefooted outside? When facing a serious surgery, why is it important to laugh? What is a "sugar stop," and what do you do there?

We spent a lot of time waiting in Mama's hospital room wondering when her heart surgery would finally be confirmed. We sat in the third-floor waiting room of the Arkansas Heart Hospital in Little Rock, watching family members of other patients come and go. We kept watch in the main floor waiting room for our buzzer to alert us of news from someone from the surgery staff.

There was much waiting during the few days I was there previous to Mama's surgery, the day of the surgery, and briefly during post-surgery. It is in the waiting, wondering, and passing of time that you can learn interesting facts. As my sister, Debbie, and I sat on the main floor with Uncle Bubba and Aunt Jan (mom's younger sister), we learned when it was warm enough for a kid in south Arkansas to go barefoot outside. (Yes, I am a girl from Arkansas who now lives in Oklahoma, and I loved to go barefoot. It is okay. I have heard all the jokes.)

Uncle Bubba informed us that it was always the first day of May. He would say, "It could still be cool outside; but if it was May 1, we went barefoot, anyway."

Aunt Jan added her memory of the rules for allowing feet to be bare. She said, "When the butterflies fly around the well, then you can go barefoot."

When the butterflies do what? I laughed so hard, I about fell out of my plastic chair. But after all these years, I now know the rules.

Mama was facing very serious surgery. We all knew that. The doctors told her it would be difficult and to prepare herself for the recovery. When asked what she had to live for, she explained about wanting to live for her children, grandchildren, and her first great-grandchild to be born in the summer. She quickly added, though, that if she did not make it, she would get to go to Heaven and be with Jesus and with my daddy, who had died only eleven months earlier. She would win either way. It was serious stuff. My brother and sister and I chose not to talk about the second option and decided instead to discuss plans for Mama's rehabilitation location when she got out of the hospital.

It was serious stuff, this open-heart surgery talk of a bypass, valve replacements, and repairs. Lots of hours of surgery were performed on a little lady who was already too weak from months of not being able to breathe adequately. The serious talk did not get in the way of her sense of humor. As she lay in her hospital bed, she was asked what she needed and what we could do for her. She would calmly reply with a hint of a twinkle in her blue eyes, "Well, I'm going to go home, and you can lay in this bed." I only wish we could have.

My sister mildly reprimanded mother for not taking care of herself by eating nutritiously and that she would have to do better when she got home.

Mama replied, "Well, you just don't know how hard it is to sit down and eat by yourself."

Debbie retorted, "Then stand up and eat, Mother, if that's what it takes."

A healthy sense of humor had served all of us well as we grew up in a preacher's home. Mama had been the picture-perfect pastor's wife, serving together with her husband and taking care of her three children. But Mama said many times, "I wasn't the best preacher's wife because I couldn't play the piano." She was the model of hospitality as she could cook, clean, and decorate her house; host women's missions meetings in our home; and a myriad of other tasks that went unnoticed.

Then there was the sugar stop. As we followed the nurse as she wheeled Mama's bed toward the surgery room, she told us that there would be a sugar stop along the way. I whispered to my brother and sister to see if they knew what that was. We were all wondering if they would give us candy or if there were other treats to be offered around the next corner. That seemed unlikely, since we were in a heart hospital.

As we reached the final intersection that led to either the surgical wing or to the waiting room, the nurse said we could all take a quick moment to tell our mom goodbye and give her a kiss. We were in the South; and often, kisses are referred to as "sugar." Debbie went first and then turned quickly away to walk down the hall. It was my turn then. The bed was high; so I reached up on my tiptoes, leaned over, kissed Mama's cheek, and said, "I'll see you soon."

The next day, when the surgeon told our family she was not going to recover, I thought about the sugar stop and the words I had said. Yes, I will see her again—but a little later than I had expected. I will see her and Daddy in Heaven when God decides my work is finished here. That will be the best Sugar Stop of all.

I Know His Voice. He Knows My Name.

Can you think of a time when you were stressed, in need of calm assurance; and just at the right moment, someone you love spoke your name? In that moment, even in the chaos, you knew all would be well. I am reminded back to the days not long after Johnny and I were married. He was supposed to be on a weekend retreat with men from our church. I was sleeping soundly late one night in our apartment while he was gone, when all at once, I was startled awake. I heard the sound of our apartment door opening. We lived in a cheap building in a sketchy part of Fort Worth, Texas. A couple of flimsy locks on the door were not going to keep intruders out for long.

But before I could even barely open my eyes and be scared, I heard my name. "DeAnna, it's me. It's okay. I just decided to come home early." And all was well. It was the voice of my beloved.

There is power and peace in hearing your name spoken by someone you know and love. Even sheep know this. They do not even need to be seen to know they are loved. They just need to hear their shepherd's tender voice. John 10:3-5 tells us, "'To him the gatekeeper opens. The sheep hear his voice, and he calls his own sheep by name and leads them out. When he has brought out all his own, he goes before them, and the sheep follow him, for they know his voice. A stranger they will not follow, but they will flee from him, for they do not know the voice of strangers.'"

I know that Voice! He knows my name! Sheep are not known to be the most intelligent creatures God made. But they know the voice of their shepherd. They know when they are safe.

There are plenty of examples in Scripture of Jesus speaking someone's name:

- "When he had said these things, he cried out with a loud voice, 'Lazarus, come out'" (John 11:43).
- "And when Jesus came to the place, he looked up and said to him, 'Zacchaeus, hurry and come down, for I must stay at your house today'" (Luke 19:5).
- "Jesus said to her, 'Mary.' She turned and said to him in Aramaic, 'Rabboni!' (which means Teacher)" (John 20:16).

Can you even imagine? Mary was distraught. She did not know where they had taken Him. Then, a man she thought was the gardener simply said one word—the only word she needed to hear to bring her back into a safe place. He said her name. Jesus said to her, "Mary." And she knew. She was flooded with peace. She did not know what was happening, but she knew Him. He knew her name. That was enough.

You can know that in your crazy, chaotic world, He is there with you. He knows your name. He knows precisely where you are. You know His voice. Listen for it. That is enough.

When God Speaks

How does God speak to you? For me, it is in a variety of ways. Sometimes, it is through His creation. Other times, it is through other people; and often, it is through Scripture. Sometimes, He speaks through several means in a short amount of time. Maybe it is because I am stubborn and do not want to hear, so He uses repetition to get my attention.

Recently, I was reading a devotional book. Toward the end of the reading, the author said that she fully realized her temple (her body) may not be God's grandest dwelling; but she wanted to lift up to the Lord whatever willingness she had each day and dedicate all as a gift to Him and a gift to herself. In other words, she wanted to worship Him by caring for the temple He indwells now.

Later, I was editing a co-worker's newsletter, reporting about working in hard places where women and girls were abused, exploited, and impoverished. The newsletter described a common conflict in this work—how the abused reconciles with the abuser or permanently leaves the abuser, who is often a family member. The teenage girl had to learn how to define boundaries that no longer allowed her to be abused. She had come to realize that her body was a temple God had given her. She was awakening to the reality that she had value and deserved respect.

From two totally different sources, I read the same message—care for yourself because God made you, loves you, and lives within you.

As if that was not enough, the Scripture highlighted in Sunday school the next morning was Romans 12:1-2: "I appeal to you therefore, brothers, by the mercies of God, to present your bodies as a living sacrifice, holy and acceptable to God, which is your spiritual worship. Do not be conformed to this world, but be transformed by the renewal of your mind, that by testing you may discern what is the will of God, what is good and acceptable and perfect." I got the message. I may be dense sometimes, but I heard God telling me—reminding me—that He was there with me and He wanted all of me.

When I returned from Indonesia that spring, I asked people to pray for me specifically in three areas. As I had considered our She Is Safe holistic approach related to body, mind, and spirit, I felt challenged to be a healthy example in each of those areas of my life. I prayed continually that I could develop discipline in each area so that God would be honored in all I say and do.

I am reminded often when I pray that I can be the answer to my own prayers. Each day, each moment, I am to present my whole self as a living sacrifice in the choices I make, in the actions I choose, and in the words I speak. It is a challenge for all of us as we seek to see the unseen, meet them at the point of their pain, and shine the light of Christ. Every day is a new day to commit to being a living sacrifice God will use to bless others.

2
Seeing the Unseen from My Minivan

FOR MANY YEARS, I WOULD sit on the little sofa in our small front room I named "the Library," and I would sip steaming black coffee and look at the photos hanging on the wall. I lovingly called it "baby corner." They were my babies, and their pictures were hanging in the corner. They were Rachel and Johnny III's high school senior photos—really good photos of my beautiful children. My kids told me for years that I could take them down, since they did not look like that anymore; but I liked looking at my baby corner. It reminded me of days past when they lived at home instead of across town or in a different town hours away. Then when the house flooded and the remodel happened, down came the framed photos, and up went new cream-colored paint. There was no more baby corner. When the remodel was complete, we took new family photos and created a wall full of family portraits.

The funny thing is, this wall faces the former baby corner in the same room. Just a short trip away from their high school years, my kids are young adults. They are all grown up. How did that happen? My son graduated two more times since the years that made the baby corner and has now launched his professional counseling career. He married and gave us three beautiful grandchildren. My daughter married and has two of her own daughters now. The number of photos on the family photo wall continues to grow.

Each year, during graduation season, I see on social media all the photos of caps and gowns and celebrations and plans for the future. We receive several graduation announcements each year. My uncle beautifully framed my kids' announcements and photos, and they were hanging in our hallway for many years until the aforementioned remodeling and painting.

To all my friends who have graduating seniors that you recently photographed and celebrated, please be aware, it is a short trip from the baby corner to the family wall. It happens very quickly. Soon, your family will grow, and you will be packing away old photos and making room on your wall for children-in-law and grandchildren. So seize the moments. Life will bring challenges. It will bring worries. It will bring opportunities to go to places across the ocean. But today, be present in the moment. Your mission today is to see the people around you in this moment in time.

Take a lot of photos and cry and remember when you dropped them off at kindergarten for the first day. Soon you will be dropping them off for their college freshman year. It is okay. You can cry a little. Take a few moments to celebrate yourself as a parent. It was you who drove them to school all those years. It was you who made sure their homework was complete, and it was you who sat in parking lots waiting for the school bell to ring or waiting for soccer practice to be over for another day. It is okay. Celebrate the moments.

As grandmother times five, I feel like I have earned the right to tell you to enjoy your children at every phase of life. Do not wish away any phase of life, even if it is the challenging toddler years or explosive teenage years. You do not get those years back. Savor them. Treasure them in your heart. And remember, it is a short trip from the baby corner to the family wall.

Mom, Are You Worrying?

My son would ask me often during his growing-up years, "Mom, are you worrying?" He could tell when I was overwhelmed with the worries of the day—whether it was big worries, like who was going to win the current presidential race, or little worries, like what to cook for dinner.

I came by my problem honestly. I only had to look at my immediate family's background to see that I had inherited my worrying gene from a long line of worriers—my mother and her mother before her. They were good, sweet, wonderful women. I am grateful they are my heritage. Yet they tended to default to worry first before considering other ways to handle perplexing situations.

I remember when I was worried about my twelve-year-old black Labrador, Pepper. She was not feeling well, and I worried if she would make it through the night before I could get her to the vet. The next morning, she was much improved. My husband teased me that I should worry more often, since apparently, all is well the next morning if I worry all night.

I internalize my worry. From the outside, as you view my approach to life, you would observe that I am mostly calm and look at situations positively. I am not a negative person. I like to see the best in people, and one of my favorite words is hope. I expect that good will overcome evil. It seems I do a great job of hiding my doubts.

I have never been in despair as some people live. I have never seriously thought of taking my own life, as is the case with many people. During a trip to Indonesia, I was reminded of the cloud of hopelessness many people live under each day. This remains the case for many unseen women in Sumatra. They chose to end their own life instead of living each day worrying if they would have enough money to buy food for their children, or if their drunken husbands would beat them or one of their children that day, or if they mattered to anyone at all.

That was the situation of my friend I met several years ago when she was only seventeen and pregnant. Her husband beat her every day, and she was concerned about the health of her unborn child. A couple of years later, her situation had not improved; and my young friend was prepared to end her life because her husband would not stop his cruel mistreatment of her. He continued to beat her and endangered her life and the life of her little boy. She was pregnant again. She was prepared to escape her misery by swallowing fertilizer and dying. She stopped herself as she remembered the needs of her son and that many people were praying for her. Today, she has a healthy son and daughter. Her smile proves that she does not worry anymore about whether she should live or die; and she knows for sure her life does matter to God, her family, and her women's support group. She feels seen and loved.

Recently, I read two books at the same time (not unusual for me at all, but normally it is five or more). I read *Prayer* by Timothy Keller and *To Fly Again: Surviving the Tailspins of Life* by Gracia Burnham. In the first book, I highlighted the sentence, "We are to pray with confidence and hope . . . to say, here's what I need—but You know best."[1] There is not a word in there about telling God what I need and then to start worrying about it as if He never heard me. In the second book, written by the missionary survivor of a year-long captivity in the Philippines in which her husband was killed, Gracia devoted an entire chapter to "Worry Doesn't Help." She cited Philippians 4:6-7: "Do not be anxious about anything, but in everything by prayer and supplication with thanksgiving let your requests be made known to God. And the peace of God, which surpasses all understanding, will guard your hearts and your minds in Christ Jesus." She had much to worry about during her year in the steamy jungles. Were her children okay? What about their missionary work? Was it continuing? When would they ever be rescued? These were all legitimate worries, yet she concluded, "God is in charge, and we are not. If he doesn't need to worry about the current state of affairs (and he doesn't), then neither do we."[2]

Many of us are worried right now about the state of our nation and our world. I am not in despair over it, but it does make me question what our future holds. There are legitimate concerns and perhaps much to worry about.

---

1 Timothy Keller, *Prayer: Experiencing Awe and Intimacy with God* (New York: Penguin Books, 2016), 101.
2 Gracia Burnham, *To Fly Again: Surviving the Tailspins of Life* (Carol Stream: Tyndale House Publishers, Inc., 2006), 66.

But do we blast social media with our worries, or do we pray? Do we watch endless news reports about the current messiness of our world, or do we hope in the Lord? Do we morph into despair and ignore what we can do to help, or do we say to the Lord, "You are in control. Use me as your agent of change"?

The answer I most often gave my son was, "Yes. I'm worrying. Even though I shouldn't, I am." I would look at his smiling face and remember that I, too, should have the faith of a child to know that God is in control and there is no need to worry.

Worry, Part Two

Twenty-five years have passed since my sweet little boy asked me if I was worrying. Yet I am still trying to get a handle on my worrying problem today. I could blame my mother, or her mother, or her mother before her. I have never done the ancestry test that is so popular now, but I am 100 percent sure that my DNA would clearly identify the worry gene originated all the way back to Ireland and England hundreds of years ago.

I wish I could dump all the blame on them or on the way God made me. Yet I take responsibility and also made sure I passed my well-earned anxieties to my daughter and, most likely, to at least one of my granddaughters. Old habits die hard, it seems.

I have gotten some great advice on how to overcome my natural bent toward stress and anxiety:

- Take deep breaths.
- Go for a walk.
- Pray and meditate.
- Pet my dog.
- Take medication.
- Just get over it. You have a great life. There is nothing at all to worry about.

All of these pieces of advice have merit, except maybe the last one, which is not helpful at all. To be honest, I have tried them all. Yet here I am, worried about why I worry so much. I worry about why I wake up consistently at 3:00 a.m., worry for a few hours, and then fall into an exhausted sleep. I worry when I travel away from the safety of home—away from dependable, clean restrooms and into the unknown.

Not long ago, I led my adult Bible study class through the book of Hebrews. Each chapter is rich with meaning. In chapters three and four, the writer talks about receiving God's rest. He talks about trust and peace. He tells the readers of the book to not be like the Israelites, who wandered in the desert for forty years because of their mistrust. (Did you know it could have taken them only two weeks?)

A Bible commentator I read made a quick comparison to the way we live. He called it "churning." That is his definition of what happens when you wake up and worry at 3:00 a.m. for two hours. Churning is the opposite of rest. When we worry, we are either in a panic or being prideful—or both. We are saying to ourselves, "I'm not going to make it," or "I don't need anyone's help, especially God's."

What do I do when worry wants to push down on me until I feel panicky and suffocating? What do I do when I feel like God does not see me in my distress? I pray. I ask for peace. I surrender my anxieties. (It sounds much like the list above.) The answer is, I do not need to go online and self-medicate. I need to ask the Giver of Peace for His answer. That may mean to go to the doctor and get some help. It may mean to get out my journal and write out my troubles and my prayers. It always means to "be still and know" (Psalm 46:10) that He has got this. And He has got me.

As I prepared to travel for several days, I felt a bit of anxiety creeping in. But as I started to worry, I remembered reading, "Thus says the Lord: 'Stand by the roads, and look, and ask for the ancient paths, where the good way is; and walk in it, and find rest for your souls'" (Jer. 6:16). It sounds like a good theme verse for a journey. I will add it to the other verses about trust and casting my cares on Him (1 Peter 5:7). I will also pack a stress ball, some calming music on my playlist, and some extra melatonin—along with nighttime acetaminophen and anti-nausea medication.

What about you? How do you answer the question, "Are you worrying?" What unseen issues have you struggled with for many years? What unseen issues are you dealing with today?

Am I a Terrible Mother?

It was back-to-school time. I noticed it first when the local superstore put out the school supply lists and all the items for parents to buy were strategically placed as shoppers came in the front entrance. Silently, I rejoiced. "Yay! Children are going back to school in just a few weeks!" Why did that elicit such a joyous response in me? I did not have school-aged children anymore. I have not had them in a very, very long time. Now, I have school-aged grandchildren. Why this response at my golden age of life?

It started when I did have grade-school children. I would purchase all those needed supplies—backpacks and lunchboxes, pencils and crayons, new clothes and shoes. On and on the list went. Then the morning came— the first day of the fall semester. I transported them to their new classrooms and scurried back to my car.

While other moms were weepy and sad to have their babies away from them the whole day, what did I do? I met a friend at a nearby restaurant. She had just dropped her children off at their school as well. We ordered breakfast and enjoyed a leisurely time together, sipping our coffee and not hearing the sounds of school-aged children scurrying about. Then what did I do? I went to the grocery store and did my shopping in a very calm atmosphere, free from the sounds of harried mothers loudly correcting their children and reminding them, "No! We can't buy that toy. We need to get everything on this school list. Just where are the colored pencils?" Then I went home, made myself another cup of coffee, went out to my back porch, and enjoyed the quiet. Ahhh. I breathed deeply and was just still.

Does that make me a terrible mother? Do not get me wrong. I love my children. We had a great time through their growing-up years going to the library, reading books, playing ball, and watching children's shows. Again, do not get me wrong, I do not enjoy being with everyone's children. I do not normally sign up for extra nursery or children's church duty. I was not the hovering classroom mom who boarded yellow school buses and went on field trips to the zoo or parks or county fairs. I was thankful other moms loved to do that. It was not me.

Does that make me a terrible mother? I was the mom who signed up every year to make pink iced Valentine's cookies with red sprinkles. I was the mom who made sure my two kids did their homework, were on time to school, and sent teacher gifts at Christmas. I was the mom who signed up to work with teenagers, not children, at church. When I got too old to be patient with teenagers, I was the mom who signed up to teach adult Sunday school and took everyone on mission trips. So, that is me—an introverted mom who loved her children but enjoyed the moments of quiet at home to do my projects, writing, and work. I was the mom who let her kids sign up for only one other extracurricular activity in addition to church things. I just did not want us all to be crazy busy. I was the mom who made sure we ate as many dinners together at the table as we could, even when the kids could drive and wanted to be twelve other places.

If all of that makes me a terrible mom, then so be it. It probably means I will be the grandmother who does not organize elaborate arts and crafts projects or have them sleep over every weekend. I will have them come, and we will be together and read books and color pages and tell stories. Then I will send them home. Occasionally, we will have a weekend together in our home. I still enjoy my peace. I am still introverted. I still love my children and grandchildren.

I am good with that. I will smile when I see a school bus roll by my window, yet enjoy the less-crowded and much more peaceful shopping experience. I will go home and enjoy my coffee on my back porch and just be still.

A Family of Nons

Several years ago, before my children started their families, I paused to consider my little family and realized that three of the four people in my family worked for nons—nonprofit organizations. At that point, I had worked for She Is Safe for two years. Then both of my children started working for nonprofit organizations as well.

Johnny III worked for a children's outreach nonprofit ministry in Oklahoma City after he received his master's degree in counseling from the University of Oklahoma. Did it surprise me that a very smart, educated, and humble young man worked for an organization dedicated to helping inner-city children know each week that they were loved, seen, and needed? I was not surprised at all. We knew he could work toward establishing his lucrative private counseling practice, and maybe he would one day. But at that time, the kid with a soft heart and a humble spirit was spending time with at-risk kids and enlisting volunteers to invest their time into the lives of children who would otherwise be overlooked. This was the same young man who spent a few weeks in Haiti following the massive earthquake in 2010, caring for orphans and pouring his life into theirs so they would know they were not alone. God could do great things with a young man with a clear vision and a heart to serve others.

Rachel, my firstborn, had always had a soft heart for children. I remembered the photo of her on a trip to northern Mexico when she was in high school. She seemed completely at home in another culture surrounded by children smiling and speaking Spanish. This was the same girl in college who spent two weeks in South Africa among underserved orphaned children who needed to be shown unconditional love.

I remembered many years ago making weekly trips with Rachel and a group of young teenage girls from our church to visit Gabriel's House, a local after-school ministry to children. Rachel returned to this organization after college graduation to work as a site assistant coordinator for a semester. Then she married and moved away to start a new life with her husband. When Rachel and her family moved back to her hometown, she was once again employed in the same position at the same Gabriel's House.

How did we find our way to work in nonprofit organizations, where the pay was not a lot? We did it because it was a calling, not because of a paycheck. I recently read these words from the book *Love Does* by Bob Goff, and I think it explained why we found ourselves serving in nonprofit ministries. "We are doing something that involves choosing something that lights you up . . . Something you think is beautiful or lasting and meaningful." Goff says to pick something "you aren't just able to do; instead, pick something you feel like you were made to do."[3] Part of that calling meant you desired to see unseen, overlooked people in your work and as you go throughout your day. I think that is why my son, my daughter, and I chose to work at nonprofit agencies that are impacting the world and making a difference.

There has been a joke in my family about my husband, the only one in my family working for profit. He has been an engineer in the same energy-based company for over thirty-five years. We say that he worked to fund my missions habit. It is true. All of our married life, I have worked for three organizations that have not paid me much money but that have enabled me to live out my calling to serve God and serve others. I am profoundly grateful for a man who not only funded my calling but supported me, encouraged me, and stayed home alone sometimes for weeks at a time so I could chase my call on the other side of the world. Thank goodness that at least one of my family members worked for profit because his dedication and hard work

---

3   Bob Goff, *Love Does: Discover a Secretly Incredible Life in an Ordinary World* (Nashville: Thomas Nelson, 2012), 216.

were invested in my work in Indonesia and our children's work in Oklahoma City and our hometown. He worked for profit to give us a comfortable life and allowed us both to serve locally in our church and community. I think his work was a calling, too. And now we get to invest in a new generation and encourage our grandchildren to dream big and follow God and their heart into the world—and sometimes, that means not for profit. Sometimes, that means seeing the unseen.

(Update: God has a way of changing our lives and putting us where we can best serve Him. As of this writing, the three of us "nons" own our businesses. I wrote content for nonprofits and then became an author. My daughter has an online crochet business, and my son has an online counseling service. My husband, the only "for profit" among our family for thirty-five years, is now officially retired and still supporting me as I write this book.)

It's a Girl!

We celebrated the happy news together. It's a girl! We learned that our second grandchild was a girl. She would soon join big sister, Leah, later that summer. This news came on International Women's Day, which reminded me that this is not news that is greeted with great joy in many places around the world. In fact, it was one reason why I had focused the last several years of my life advocating for abused and trafficked women and girls around the world.

As we ate our iced cookie cake, celebrating a new little girl, other girls around the world were aborted, abandoned, married off way too early, tricked into slavery, and physically and sexually abused. I was so thankful on the International Day for Women and throughout the year that organizations like She Is Safe were making a difference. As I looked into the eyes of my daughter, my granddaughter, and the sonogram photo of my second granddaughter, I was deeply thankful that they were loved, protected, and safe.

Take the time now to thank God for the women and girls in your life. And take a moment to pray for the many women and girls tonight that are not wanted, fed, or protected. Pray for them not to be discarded and disgraced but to be seen, safe, and loved.

So Many Riches—So Many Cucus

My first grandson, Elijah, came into the world recently. He joined our three other blessings—his cousins Leah and Alex and his big sister Natalie. Imagine the three most beautiful girls ages seven, four, one-and-a-half, and a newborn boy. I shared a photo of all my grandchildren with the She Is Safe ministry partner in Sumatra, Indonesia, with whom I had worked closely for over seven years. She sent me back a written message and also a recorded message. She wrote, "Wow! What good news. I am so happy, happy. Thanks to God. He gives us so many blessings. He likes for us to be joyful in His grace. Congratulations, happy grandmother."

In my mind, I saw her smiling face as she sent this recorded message, "Hi, DeAnna. I'm surprised! Really surprised. So many *cucu* [Indonesian word for grandchildren that sounds like *choo-choo*]. At first, you came and said *satu cucu* [one] and then *dua* [two] and, suddenly, so many *cucus* [*empat*—four—to be exact.] So many blessings. So many riches. Thank you for asking about us. We are good. Fine. Everybody asking about you and missing you. Send blessing to all of your family. Especially to your grandchildren."

Yes, so many blessings—so many *cucus*. Since I received that message, we have welcomed grandbaby number five, "lima," into our family. Our family continues to grow, and we are so thankful.

3
Seeing and Listening to Unseen People

I HAD A GREAT VACATION visiting family. Part of that time was spent with my little family (daughter, son-in-law, son, husband, myself, plus my grand-dog and grand-kitten). We stayed five days with Rachel and Nathan when they lived in their cozy Ozark Mountains home in northwest Arkansas, surrounded by trees, hills, and streams. Together, we shopped and ate and played and hiked and laughed and went to church. Now that my children are grown and do not live at home anymore, I treasure the time we can be together. I especially loved the moments when I could steal a few minutes and chat one-on-one with each of the kids. Sweet memories were made.

We spent two days with my husband's family, which included, at times, ten people in my mother-in-law's home. We enjoyed meals together and watched basketball and softball games and went for walks together. Being part of a family is always confirming and full of joyful moments. I love these people—all of them—and felt so blessed that my life was intertwined with theirs.

Whether it was traveling on vacation or traveling with She Is Safe, I often found myself surrounded by people. It is hard to find solitude and moments of peace when you were part of a family or part of a team. That is the dilemma of an introvert—loving to be with people, yet finding your personal energy depleted by their energy. That is the best definition I have found of being an introvert—finding your energy recharged from moments of solitude and personal inward peacefulness, as opposed to an extrovert, who finds energy from being around other people. Her personal energy is depleted when she is alone and needs other people to recharge.

I find confirmation in that definition that it is okay to be an introvert in a world that seems to place more value on those who like to be the life of the party and who have never met a stranger. Somehow, our culture does not value as much those of us who need a generous amount of time reading, thinking, or just being alone. I was driven to the book, *The Introvert Advantage: How Quiet People Can Thrive in an Extrovert World* by Marti Olsen Laney. It is good to know that there is a book out there by that title. It makes me feel like I am not the only person in the world who struggles with this personality trait.

For a person like me who needs generous alone time, I still often found myself on crowded airplanes on international flights, in a hotel room with a teammate, in front of a group giving a presentation, or in a house full of family. I was okay with that because I knew when I came home, my personal sanctuary awaited with plenty of quiet places to welcome me—on my walks alone with my music, on my back porch with just me and my dogs, or in my office with my books and my laptop, surrounded by art and maps and trinkets I have collected from my global journeys. In the evenings, when Johnny came home from work, we enjoyed our quiet evenings and settled into a routine that included together time with our two Labradors.

I soaked in the solitude and prepared myself for opportunities of sharing life with others God had put into my life. I was happy for that balance and grateful for the quiet moments alone, as well as for the activities full of the sounds of life spent with family, friends, and strangers. I was grateful for the people God had put into the world and that introverts need extroverts and vice versa. I was thankful that I have grown into the place in my life where I can appreciate those who are different from me and thankful for the person God has made me to be. I am thankful that He sees us all and made us differently by His holy design.

I can be a traveling introvert and absorb the sights and sounds and new experiences that life offers and appreciate all that later when those experiences are a memory. Then, when I am alone again, I can take time to reflect, remember, and share with others the journal of a traveling introvert and the great places I have been honored to go and the great people I have been privileged to meet. I love appreciating and sharing the notes and the rests that make up the music of life.

Ears to Hear Everywhere You Go

"'He who has ears to hear, let him hear'" (Matt. 11:15). I heard it three times within a few days. Once a month, the She Is Safe International Ministries team met together via electronic devices and shared updates, news, and prayers. One week, our India team reported on their recent trip. The staff member tasked with teaching women business skills told us about the training she had implemented with women who were already small business owners. At the end of the interactive training that week, they evaluated together what they had learned.

One woman told our She Is Safe staff member, "I like it when you ask us questions. It makes us think."

Knowing my friend, I knew she had listened to their concerns and followed up with more questions. Have ears to hear everywhere you go.

The next week, I hosted our She Is Safe advocacy team in my home. We had a good time together eating Christmas snacks, laughing, and praying—and doing lots of talking. We discussed upcoming plans for our team, but we also spent time catching up with each other. We just enjoyed being together. When most of the women had left, a few remained and continued to chat with each other. I noticed two of them were talking a lot. Later, the one answering most of the questions told me about her sister advocate, "She asks great questions. And she listened. I like that about her." Have ears to hear everywhere you go.

Not all of the lessons I learned about listening during those weeks were positive. In the middle of one of my conversations, the person I was speaking to abruptly interrupted my words and interjected what was on her mind. She gave no apology—not an "I'm sorry to interrupt you; what were you saying?" From that encounter, it was clear to me what that person wanted to say was more important than listening to my thoughts. Have ears to hear everywhere you go.

As an introvert, I am used to not always being heard. I read the book, *Quiet: The Power of Introverts in a World That Can't Stop Talking* by Susan Cain. Sometimes, we all feel like what we have to say must be heard loudly and immediately. But if we are all talking, who is listening?

Part of my job when I served as the She Is Safe country director for Indonesia involved interviewing women and girls to hear their stories. When I first began the job, I was overwhelmed by the task of getting good information. In advance, I wrote a long list of questions so I would make sure I could keep the conversations flowing. Years later, I continued to travel to remote, unseen villages and gathered with women on the floors of their homes and asked questions. I had learned that it was not in the volume of questions that I asked, but powerful stories came from asking the right questions. Only a few were necessary. Then it was time to just listen. As the interpreter told me the answers of each woman and girl, my challenge was to listen, absorb her words and what she was saying, and then form another question. It seems easy enough, but it was extremely challenging.

Our Wednesday night church discipleship group had been reading and discussing a book called *The Insanity of God* by Nik Ripken. Nik was a missionary who took several years to interview Christians who were going through persecution or who had successfully endured it. He traveled to big cities as well as remote locations in Russia, Ukraine, China, and many other restricted and dangerous areas of the world. His purpose was to learn about how to endure persecution so he could share his findings with others who could then be prepared to undergo persecution when it came. What Nik learned as he talked to hundreds of people was that the benefit of what he was doing was not in the advice he could offer people. The true benefit of his interviews came in the power of the stories of each person as they spoke and he listened. Yes, he learned many things about thriving in times of torture and imprisonment, but he did not first list those things for us to read. He first shared their stories—powerful, life-changing stories. The sequence was important. First, he had to go, and then he had to listen.[4] Have ears to hear wherever you go.

We all need to talk. We all need to listen. And when we speak, we want to be heard. In addition to encouraging you to go to unseen places, my challenge to all of us is to give the gift of listening to someone who needs to be heard.

What to Do on a Staycation

I desperately needed to do nothing—or as close to nothing as possible. I had no desire to get on a plane or in a car and travel somewhere. My work gave me plenty of opportunities to do that. I needed to be still and enjoy some long, uninterrupted peace and quiet. On the last day of my self-proclaimed stay-at-home vacation, it was time to evaluate my week and discover if it was worth it before the work week began again.

Do not get me wrong—I loved my work. I found meaning and purpose in being part of an organization that helped bring freedom and hope globally to enslaved and abused women and girls. However, at some point, it became a lot—a lot of darkness, a lot of organizing, a lot of awareness and fundraising, a lot of travel. It was time to step away, if only for a week and if only to my back porch or across town.

On Monday, I took my coffee, e-reader, a journal, a Bible, and, of course, my dogs, Daisy and Rosie, and walked out my back door. I spent a lot of time all week enjoying the August mornings on my porch drinking coffee, reading, and journaling. If I did nothing but this all week, it would have been fine

---

4 Nik Ripken, *The Insanity of God: A True Story of Faith Resurrected* (Nashville: Broadman and Holman Publishers, 2013).

with me. I looked up through the trees and let God speak. I did not ask for much, just to enjoy the view. I was determined not to read articles or books about subjects related to sexual abuse or human trafficking. I needed to fill my heart with hope and goodness and light. When I was ready to come inside, my view was more puppies and more coffee. It may not sound very exciting, but that is exactly what my soul needed.

I knew I still needed to walk and care for my health; so on Tuesday, I headed across town to a park. I walked and sweated for a while and then read and journaled and drank lots of water. My view expanded to watching geese swim about on the small pond. It was refreshing. Of course, I would be lying if I did not confess that I binged on Netflix often throughout the week. It was mind-numbing, and that was exactly what I needed mentally. To make sure I kept my mind relaxed, I downloaded the sounds of white noise and nothingness. That was what my soul was thirsty for.

One of my easy-to-accomplish goals for the week was to visit a couple of local coffee shops, take my e-reader, read, and take time to relax and not worry about keeping appointments and organizing trips or events. I did all of that in two coffee shops in town. They made my favorite hot beverage—a tall skinny vanilla latte. I know how to live large.

There was one day out of the week I took time to be Bebe (my granddaughter's name for me), and that same day had to deal with stresses brought on by a roofing contractor. Throughout the week, I still had to prepare meals and wash some dishes and do loads of laundry. But those stresses were short-lived; and I quickly got back to reading, drinking coffee, walking, praying, and doing nothing. I was getting remarkably good at it.

Then Friday arrived. Without even thinking, I naturally clicked on some articles about helping abused women who lived in unseen shame-based cultures. This is what much of my She Is Safe work dealt with, and then I watched a video about this issue. Then I read another article about abuse. What was happening here? I swore I would step away from it for just one week. I could not do it. It is not that I planned it. It came instinctively. It is just who I was. This made me realize, it was time to go back to work. It was so confirming and encouraging to know it was time to continue on my journey.

What do you do on a staycation? You do nothing. Get rested. Recharged and relaxed, you then get ready to go back to doing what you were made to do. First, maybe take one more quick nap.

Where I Meet God

I have said it before. One of my favorite places in the world is right outside my back door, where my view of my backyard is from my rocking chair. I have had many worship-filled mornings meeting God on my back porch in the cool and quiet with my coffee and dogs. Only the birds supplied a background concert of morning praise.

While this was my morning routine when I was home each day, every Sunday morning took me to a house of worship. As the daughter of a pastor, I have worshiped in many churches. Since I was born over sixty years ago, I have been a member of at least seventeen Baptist churches—small country churches, large city churches, medium small-town churches. I have sung hymns and choruses and heard choir anthems, pipe organs, guitars, and drums. I have sung out of hymnals, from words projected on the wall, and from copies of both hymns and choruses. And while I have loved these churches and the people in them, when I think of meeting God in worship, my mind immediately goes to these unseen places:

- In a small garage behind a home in South Africa, a single light bulb swayed in the breeze; and in the coolness of a June evening, we huddled together to sing praise and share testimonies of God's grace.
- In a home in Mexico, we ate a home-cooked meal that included handmade tortillas, and we broke into song with the words of

"Amazing Grace" in Spanish and English melded together to offer up a sweet aroma to our shared Maker.

- During a Sunday morning service in northeastern Bangladesh, our mission team, who had not been in the country very long, with heavy eyes and jetlag almost taking over tried to engage in the music and sermon all presented in Bengali. We continually punched each other to keep our eyes open. I remembered how amazing it was to feel so at home and welcomed on the other side of the world with people worshiping the same God I knew. It did not matter that we could not understand a single word. God was there with us. He accepted our worship in whatever language we offered.
- In Rome on a Sunday morning, we attended an English service, so we could understand and participate. What I most remembered was that most of us were visitors to that country; yet wherever our home nation was, it did not matter. We all worshiped the same God. I remembered a visiting handbell choir. As they played, the acoustics of the ancient building captured the musical praise and offered it Heavenward.
- In the country of Indonesia, sitting in the home of my co-worker and host, I joined with many of our fellow workers and believers, who had gathered to sing together and pray for one another. It was their custom to pray aloud. The noise was loud at first, as many voices in both English and Bahasa Indonesian were offered to God all at the same time. Sometimes, I was quiet and just listened to the passion in the voices as my Indonesian friends prayed. They knew God heard, and they prayed with all their heart and soul.

Back in my home church when I returned to the States, I reentered the familiarity of the music, the order of worship and sermon, the ability to understand all the words and feel comfortable and part of the family. Sometimes, as I sat in my beautiful church building, I remembered where I had been and how it did not matter that I could not speak the language, or know the words of the songs, or read the Scripture in a different language. It did not matter; the ways of worship were unimportant—what we sang, which Bible versions we used, or what we were wearing—as we sat in our buildings. It did not matter the "where" of worship—whether in Indonesia; Rome, Italy; or Duncan, Oklahoma on my back porch—God was with us. It was all about Him. That was enough.

Did You Hear That?

Listen. Did you hear that? Nothing? Exactly. I take that back. I heard the wind through the trees and autumn leaves wisping to the ground. I heard the solo of a bird chirping nearby. It was music to my soul—the quiet, the coolness, the nothingness of being still.

Even though I had been a wandering sojourner most of my life, I had entered a new season. Just as summer had slipped into autumn, so had I sensed the altering of time. Even though my job had changed and did not require as much travel, I was eager to know when I could go again, envious of my friends and co-workers making their plans and packing their bags, while my itinerary was empty, just like my suitcases.

I grew up in an evangelical denomination. It had been our heart's cry to go into all the world and preach, to go and help, to go and learn, to just go. So I did. For thirty years, I traveled locally and globally because of this call on my life. It was a good call—a godly call.

Then, on an ordinary morning a few days ago, sitting in my comfy chair reading, drinking coffee, and contemplating life, I heard something. It was a whisper, but I heard it.

"It's okay to spend some time with Me. It's okay to be still." Then it was quiet.

I did not say, "What was that? Can you say that again please a little louder? I didn't hear you," because I did. The truth had already sunk deep into my soul. "Just be still for a season and listen. It's okay to enjoy Me."

I could have argued with God. "There is too much to do. So many people who do not know You. There are so many women and girls trapped in the darkness of abuse and slavery. There is so little time to go and rescue them."

It is true. Yet it is not all up to me. This is His world and His battle; and when He said it was time to be still, it meant He had it under control. He was calling others to answer the command to go. It did not mean He would not call again for me to pack my bags and go, but for now, it was time to be still and worship and know Him. It was a time for me to enjoy the moments and soak up the quiet, to take a journey to nowhere.

Hope in a New Year

It started with my Sunday school teacher and friend, Jamie, challenging our small group to prayerfully select a word that would represent our theme for the coming year. That is where the obsession with the word *hope* began. It changes everything. Without it, the light goes out of our eyes. There is no need to go on. What point is a new year when hope fades?

I even purchased a wood carving of the word *hope* and placed it by my globe. He really is the Hope for the world. Scripture is full of hope from the Psalms to the New Testament letters: "And now, O Lord, for what do I wait? My hope is in you" (Psalm 39:7). "Blessed be the God and Father of our Lord Jesus Christ! According to his great mercy, he has caused us to be born again to a living hope through the resurrection of Jesus Christ from the dead, to an inheritance that is imperishable, undefiled, and unfading" (1 Peter 1:3-4).

Do a search in your Bible. You will discover so many words and stories of hope. Where would Abraham have been without hope when he started on his journey into the unknown, the unseen, to go to the place where God was leading him? Where would Mary have been without hope when the angel revealed God's plan for a Baby for her and a Savior for all of us? Hope gives us the courage to hang on when waiting for a diagnosis, for healing, for a job, for what to do next.

My work with She Is Safe was all about giving hope to women and girls who did not know that God knew them and loved them, regardless of the person who continually abused them, regardless of the job they were forced to do every night multiple times with men who used them and left them alone, regardless of the disease they then had that affected every part of their lives and left them abandoned by their families. My family gives me much hope for each day. Watching three granddaughters and two grandsons grow and experience life brings laughter, wonder, and joy. Watching both my son and daughter weave their way through life with their spouses brings a sense of completion and hope in my life knowing they have chosen well.

Here are the prayers of hope I desire to pray each day, throughout the days of each new year:

- "Jesus, take control. Take over. My hope is in You."
- "Jesus, lead my family. My hope is in You."
- "Jesus, lead my work. My hope is in You."
- "Jesus, lead my marriage. My hope is in You."
- "Jesus, lead my life. My hope is in You."

What word will you choose to be your theme for the year? Maybe it is *joy*, or *dare*, or *dream*, or *love*. Whatever it is for you, my hope for you is that in each new year, you know that God is with you and that He loves you completely and without condition. It is a hope you can count on.

4
Seeing People Virtually

MY BRAND NEW LAPTOP FINALLY arrived. It was beautiful beyond description. I spend a lot of time with my laptop. It is what writers do. When the laptop you have had for several years decides that it is done with you, it is a sad day. That is what happened before my annual work retreat. My laptop gave up the ghost. My techy son-in-law tried to revive it, and not even he could resurrect it. It was hopeless.

Sadly, I left for my retreat laptop-less. It was not a pretty picture. While there, I received a message from my husband that he had ordered me a new one. Oh, happy day! I envisioned arriving home the following week and getting acquainted with my new best friend. Alas, when I got home, I learned that the package had not even shipped yet. So I suffered. And I waited.

My work went on, even though I remained without a laptop. I used my other devices: my tablet, my very old desktop computer, and my smartphone. There were so many electronics; yet still, I suffered—or so it seemed.

It took a full two weeks to receive my new laptop. Can you imagine? I was conditioned to deliveries in two days. Oh, happy day when the delivery truck finally arrived with my prized possession. I was no longer suffering as I wrote daily on my new keyboard. We have since spent a whole lot of time together. It is a beautiful thing, suffering no more.

Hopefully, you get my point. I know nothing of suffering, not really. I remember a few years ago sitting in the home of our Sumatra Indonesia ministry partner. She asked me to join her with her guest, who sat quietly, humbly in her living room. She asked me to meet with him and hear his story. As I listened, I knew there was no way I could enter his world and know his pain. He had spent the last nine years in jail, where his crime did not fit his punishment. While he was imprisoned, his captors pulled off his fingernails and toenails in an attempt to get him to reveal other believers in the area. In excruciating pain, he refused to talk. One by one, his nails were ripped off. Infection followed. While he was away, his son was born—a son he did not meet until he was released only a few days before. How could I pray for him when my idea of suffering was waiting for a delayed delivery?

I have experienced loss—my dad, my mom, and a ministry job. All of it was painful. We all go through the valleys that life brings. There was the suffering of my friend and coworker, Cherylann, who lost her battle with colorectal cancer. There was the suffering of my friend and coworker, Daniel, who dealt with chemo and hospitals and pain. He had a rare form of cancer that he and his family endured. His battle ended in death within a few years of his diagnosis. Together, they suffered.

Ultimately, there was the suffering of Jesus for all of us. In comparison, none of us know the depth of His suffering. As each Good Friday and Easter morning arrive, we are reminded of what the passion of Christ looked like; but we cannot know it. He took the suffering on Himself, so we would no longer need to carry the weight of it. He suffered for us all. Our suffering is brief, momentary. Is it painful? Yes, but when He said, "It is finished," He meant it. His suffering was over, as will ours be one day. We will suffer no more together. Oh, what a happy day that will be.

Virtual Home Work

"So where do you work?" It was a normal small talk-type of question that came up often in casual conversation.

When I answered, I normally would say something like, "I work for an international nonprofit organization. We help women and girls who are abused and exploited in difficult places around the world. I am the country director for Indonesia. Our office is based in Atlanta, but I get to work from my home."

"Work from home?" they usually said. "I bet that's cool." (This was in the pre-Covid years when working from home was not commonplace.)

It was cool, except when it was not. Many days, my morning schedule looked something like this:

> *6:00 a.m.*: Quiet time and coffee, breakfast, walk, shower, get dressed, more coffee.
>
> *9:00 a.m.*: Time to get to work. I sat in my swivel chair and turned on the desktop computer. While it was booting up, I ran to start a load of laundry. Finally, the computer screen popped up, and I pulled up my email. After several emails were answered, articles read, and Facebook posts updated, it was time to get to work. But first, I needed another cup of coffee; and then I would work on that report.
>
> *10:00 a.m.*: Walk out to the mailbox. Put on another load of laundry, then time to work. But wait; if we were going to have potato soup for lunch, I needed to peel potatoes and put them on to boil. Then back to work.
>
> *10:30 a.m.*: I finally pulled out the reports to work on after answering a phone call, letting the dogs out, and answering twelve texts from a variety of people. Now where was my research for this report?
>
> *11:00 a.m.*: Research found, dogs let back in, potatoes ready to chop and finish prep for soup.
>
> *11:30 a.m.*: First section of the report ready to complete.
>
> *12:00 p.m.*: Lunch with husband.

My morning was gone. The afternoon usually included errands, house cleaning, finishing laundry, preparing to teach a church class, taking my dog, Daisy, on therapy dog visits, babysitting my granddaughter, dinner prep, and more coffee. Somehow, miraculously, my work did happen. I did have time to prepare for presentations and special events. I organized trips to Indonesia. I went on those trips, returned, and recuperated from those trips. I wrote reports about those trips, prepared, wrote, rewrote, and distributed prayer letters. I read books and articles related to our work. I talked with co-workers in Atlanta, California, Indonesia, and various other locations. I attended online meetings—and I drank coffee.

I loved it all. I loved this work of helping unseen women and girls find freedom and hope. I loved to travel and visit with friends and co-workers in Indonesia, and I loved to come home and communicate with others about this amazing work. I loved to sit in my cozy home office, once my daughter's bedroom, in my swivel chair and prepare all of this amazing work. Sometimes, because I worked from home, when the weather was nice, I would take my laptop and sit on the deck in my rocking chair and enjoy the breeze, the birds, the trees, and sun. When it was cold, I could sit on the loveseat in the front room with my dogs and read from my e-reader. Sometimes, I organized events and prepared presentations while sitting in my comfy brown recliner in the living room. Usually, my work found me in the pastel blue home office lined with treasures I have brought home from my global travels.

I loved it all. Yes, it was a cool job that I did. Now, it is time to get back to work; but first, I need to get dinner started and have one more cup of coffee.

IDC Friday

It is official. It is IDC Friday—another "I Don't Care" day. Let me explain, and maybe you will want to join me in celebrating this important event. It all began in my past life when I was a part-time church staff member. As church staff members know, Sunday is a work day, since you are on call to attend to every need and person related to the church on that "day of rest." Obviously, Sunday was not a day of rest for ministers. As a preacher's kid, I knew what Sunday was—a worship service or two, plus lots of meetings, and fried chicken or pot roast for lunch.

So, church staff were urged to take another day of the week, in addition to Saturday, for time off away from the job. Early on, in my almost ten years in church missions ministry, I selected Friday. It worked well for me, and I kept that day as my official day off unless I was traveling with a missions team or there were other job assignments that had to be done that day.

As the years went by, the job challenges increased; and so did my bad attitude. I did not really know that God was unsettling me to help me release my church position and take another ministry assignment. My job as missions minister on church staff was to care about the hurt and underserved people both locally and globally and then to connect our church members to meet these needs. I needed to care about that—not just because it was my job but because it was the right thing to do. That was a big job—to care about people in need and at-risk. It was a weighty burden that needed constant attention. As time went by and my critical and tired attitude emerged, I began to care less and less about the things I should. I began to see the stresses of church challenges and difficult relationships more than I saw the needs of others outside my window. So, each Friday, I decided to put that burden and my stinky attitude down for one day—thus, the name "I Don't Care" Friday.

That was really a good thing to do. Everyone needs a sabbath. The bad thing is, sometimes your bad attitude about your job and others and life in general continue on a negative path. You may walk away from work, but you need to take up things that matter. Those things include quiet meditation time—solitude, silence, listening, praying, and praising the Maker of all things.

During recent years, I forget sometimes that I am not on a church staff and my employment continues on Fridays. When I worked virtually from my home with our She Is Safe office in Atlanta, I was also connecting online with our ministry co-workers in Indonesia. My job with She Is Safe included a lot of caring about women and girls that were abused and exploited in difficult places around the world and about weighty issues like domestic violence, physical abuse, and human trafficking. It was hard stuff that affected real people that I had met and could not forget, even on Fridays. Their pain was real and constant and blocked all hope. It was easy to get swallowed up in the darkness of it all.

Jesus said no. He did want me to care, but He wanted me to give my care to Him. Peter said, "Cast all your anxiety on him, because he cares for you" (1 Peter 5:7). Worry, sarcastic remarks, and bad attitudes were not the answer. He wanted me to rest in Him. He wanted me to let Him show me how to care for others without thinking it was up to me to save the world. That was His job. I just got to be a small part of caring for hurting, unseen people.

Taking a day off was a good thing as I shifted focus from work to worship and from completing assignments to just doing nothing. I did not have to care for work on Fridays, but I did care that others knew Him and this peace He gives. Will you join me? Today, let us lay our worries aside. That makes for a great "IDC" day every day.

How to Live and Love the Writing Life

I have not always wanted to be a writer. It was number three on my list:

1. Veterinarian
2. Artist
3. Writer
4. Cross-cultural worker

It did not take long for it to jump from number one to number two. While I loved animals, especially dogs, I learned by the time I was in the fourth grade that I did not have a scientific mind. When I found out a person had to be good at science *and* math, I began to rethink my life choices. When it dawned on me that I would have to be around bloody, diseased, sick animals all the time, I decided I would just love animals, not try to fix them.

I learned by grade six that I could draw. I could look at someone's drawings, especially cartoons, and accurately sketch them in my drawing pad. In fact, when I was in the seventh grade, I did really well in a "Draw the Picture" contest in a magazine. The company wanted me to enlist in their drawing academy—for a price, of course. My daddy said no—or, rather, not yet. I continued to draw, and I was not bad but it was hard for me to draw things from my imagination. I thought maybe that was an important part of being a successful artist.

About that time, I discovered number three: I could write. In the tenth grade, I took a creative writing class. I liked poetry of all kinds and short stories. Then I discovered journalism. I loved writing the words and sharing the words. I filled journal after journal with lots of words. I was hooked and knew this was my calling and chose communications as my major in college and graduate school. For a while, I combined number three and number four by writing for missions publications. While serving in Indonesia, I wrote the stories of at-risk women and girls. Being director of communication at She Is Safe taught me much about writing content and much about the value of nonprofits.

People think that writing is blissfully imagining characters and weaving a best-selling novel together effortlessly and that it is delightful every blessed day. Sometimes, it *is* wonderful when I sit outdoors, sip my coffee, and breathe in inspiration as the birds chirp. I savor the aroma of flowers and the fresh morning air. Sometimes, on really great days, the writing life is this for me. For those days, I am grateful.

But most days, it is more complicated. Imagine a cluttered, messy desk. I share my writing den with my lovable, goofy, sweet fox red Labradors, Cheyenne and Rosie. Sometimes, as I sit at my disordered mess of a desk, the writing life looks like taking the puppies outside, then bringing them inside, then breaking up loud dog fights, and then doing it all again. Finally, they plop down, snuggle together, and sleep sweetly on the sofa or the floor near me and snore, giving me opportunity to write. That is when I got to work on my nonprofit content writing projects. I wrote blogs, newsletters, webpage copy, grants, brochures, presentation copy, social media posts and plans, PSAs, communication strategies, stories of all kinds, and so forth.

I discovered over the past few years that I loved helping organizations that help people in a wide variety of contexts: anti-sex trafficking, children's after-school programs, food pantries, unplanned pregnancies, international job skills training and implementation. I have even written short pieces for organizations that helped children with terminal illnesses, adults with chronic autoimmune diseases, and international STEM resources for children in developing nations. Some days, my writing life included researching, learning new technology and programs, reading content-writing books and freelance business books, designing newsletters, and doing phone and personal interviews.

Living the writing life means that I drink a lot of coffee. I do enjoy sitting out on my deck and breathing in nature. It also means helping desperate young women find their way to a pregnancy resource center; informing people about how they can help prevent women from becoming trafficking victims, and teaching African young people how to develop community leaders in their own countries and improve their lives for now and the next generation. This writing life of mine is not blissful. It is hard, exhausting work. I sit with my laptop every day and write the words that provide help, hope, and encouragement. I love living this writing life. Now, back to work, right after I take the dogs outside again.

This Is My Why

"I'm a full-time writer." The first time I said it out loud was with my ladies' discipleship group. It was the first time I had introduced myself that way. Writers know it is a big deal to own who you are and let the world know it, too. It feels good to say it and to be it. Yet why do it? It does not pay very well (or at all sometimes). It is scary to write words and wonder if anyone reads them or if anyone cares. Writers write because we are driven to. We have to. It is what we do.

For me, it began as a love for reading. Some of my first memories as a child were when my brother and sister were both in school and I was home alone with

Mama all day. The doorbell rang, and the mailman had a box for us. The box label had my name printed on it. I knew what was inside. It was a brand new Dr. Seuss book. My mother had purchased a book subscription for me; and once a month, a book came to our home. Mama read that book over and over. That was just the first day I had the book. By the time my siblings got home from school, I could almost "read" the book to them myself. I loved it. I loved the smell of the new pages, the bright colors and nonsensical characters. I loved the warmth of sitting in Mama's lap as we turned the pages again and again. She even printed my name on the front of the hardcover book in permanent ink. It was all mine.

It began as a love for words and a love for books. Through the years, I have purchased and collected countless books. I have given some away and kept many. I still love the feel of a printed book in my hands.

Writing took on a serious role for me in high school when I took a creative writing class at Watson Chapel High School in Pine Bluff, Arkansas, taught by Mrs. Gorman. It changed my life. I worked on the yearbook and newspaper staff. We moved schools my senior year to El Dorado, Arkansas. That year, I wrote my own weekly newspaper column.

At Ouachita Baptist University my freshman year, my communications professor, Dr. Downs, introduced me to the five "Ws" and the "H" in Communications 101: *Who? What? When? Where? Why?* and *How?* The essentials to every good piece of journalism answered those questions in the inverted pyramid style of writing. I remember my assignments coming back all marked up in red, and I learned the tedious craft of the rewrite. I would write it again until Dr. Downs was pleased.

I loved interviewing people. I loved asking the right questions, scribbling copious messy notes, and then crafting a person's story into a publishable piece. The love for storytelling embedded itself deep into my being, and I still thrive today on hearing and telling stories.

Out in the real world, I have written feature articles for magazines, curriculum pieces for missions education organizations, and dabbled in writing a historical Christian romance novel. I even had a story printed in an edition of Chicken Soup for the Soul. I wrote a missions-themed devotional for teenage girls. I started my own blog that morphed into a weekly email newsletter. I wrote lots of stories for She Is Safe, letters, more blogs, and web copy. There were lots of words.

Why keep doing it, considering the many weeks I go unpublished or earn no money? Why do something that requires days sitting alone typing at my desk? It all boils down to it being a calling (not just because I feel like I would explode if I did not get words from my head to my fingers and to the keyboard or my journal). God equips us all with unique gifts. Sometimes, those gifts are not seen in a traditional job but come out through nurturing children, or encouraging senior adults, or making a cozy home for our families. Frederick Buechner said, "The place God calls you to is the place where your deep gladness and the world's deep hunger meet."[5]

Who Is My Audience?

That is the question I start with every time I begin writing a new piece. That is the question my journalism professors taught me to ask as I approached writing a news or feature story. That is the question I ask my clients when I begin to write content for them. Who do you expect to read this piece? What type of person is he or she? Then, when I focus on one person instead of a general lump of faceless people, my words will be sharper and make more of an impact on the reader and move her to feeling and to action.

Knowing who will read the words makes a difference in how I write the words and shape them into a story. Who are these unseen people receiving my words? Are they young? Are they old? Are they mothers or empty-nesters? Are they suffering from a disease? What is it about my audience that I need to know to make sure my words are crafted in such a way that they are

---

[5] "Vocation," The Frederick Buechner Center, July 18, 2017, https://www.frederickbuechner.com/quote-of-the-day/2017/7/18/vocation.

well-received? How can I bring my audience into better focus? It makes a difference. I noticed after I launched my freelance writing business that my focus sharpened to make sure I pleased my clients. I wanted to make them happy and give them exactly what they asked for. Of course, I did. They were the ones paying me to write what they wanted. They had become my audience.

Beyond my writing life, I wanted to please family members and help them do whatever they needed—babysit the grandchildren, go on a shopping trip, or purchase a particular type of snack for my granddaughters that they liked. I wanted to please them. Of course, I did. They were my audience and the people closest to me.

Because of my people-pleasing personality, I wanted to honor pastors and members in my church—to be the best Sunday school teacher I could be, the best discipleship group leader I could be, the best missions team leader I could be. I wanted to please them. Of course, I did. We were doing life together through our church. It was important. As I focused on doing my best for them, they became my audience.

As I looked at this list, it compelled me to say, "This is making me old and tired."

I cannot keep up. I cannot please them all—the clients, the children, the church members. If they were my audience, then I lived for their applause or encouragement from them. I wanted a "Good job, Mom. Thank you." But my number one audience is not people. It is God. It is always God. For Him alone, I do what I do. Whether it is writing, leading, or caring for my family, I should live as if my ultimate goal is always to please Him first. " . . . rendering service with a good will as to the Lord and not to man" (Eph. 6:7).

Let Me Serve You

"Here, let me serve you," or, "I'm here to serve." These are phrases I have said to family or friends when I was being silly and trying to draw attention to the fact that I was going to give extra effort to meet their needs. For example,

Unseen People

I said it when I had just gotten settled in my comfy chair and my husband asked for something from the kitchen. "I'm here to serve," I said with as much insincerity as possible and sighed a big loud sigh as I went to the kitchen to fetch his requested drink or snack or whatever. You can imagine that a sweet spirit did not fill the room.

What are serving and servanthood exactly? God has a way of getting my attention fairly often when I read the same or similar Scriptures or other readings repeatedly in a short amount of time. One morning, in two separate books, I read about Jesus serving the disciples by washing their feet in John 13. It was the very same story I read again in a different book within a matter of minutes—the picture of Jesus humbly taking the posture of a lowly servant to cleanse the dirty feet of the men who followed Him into that upper room. It was one of those moments I did not think was a random event. It made me stop and say, "Okay, God. I get it. There is something you want me to pay attention to here. What is it You desire for me to learn?" In this case, the answer was obvious. I needed to serve with the right motives. I needed to serve with joy—not because I had to, not because it made me happy, not even just to meet an immediate need or request. I needed to serve in order to bring God's joy into the situation. Mother Teresa said, "The work we do is only our love for Jesus in action."[6]

Serving comes in many forms—sometimes seen by others and sometimes not. Sometimes for me, that involves cooking and cleaning for my family. Sometimes that means praying for others. Sometimes that means traveling to the other side of the world and helping women and girls that are abused, impoverished, or exploited. Sometimes, that means taking my yellow Labrador retriever, Daisy, to the nursing home or to the hospital and providing the ministry of presence for hurt, sick, and lonely individuals. But if any of those actions are done out of obligation or in the wrong spirit, I do not receive the reward of God's joy.

---

6 "Mother Teresa Quotes," Relics World, Accessed December 9, 2022, https://www.relicsworld.com/mother-teresa.

In *One Thousand Gifts: A Dare to Live Fully Right Where You Are*, Ann Voskamp says, "Spend the whole of your one wild and beautiful life investing in many lives, and God simply will not be outdone. God extravagantly pays back everything we give away and exactly in the currency that is not of this world but the one we yearn for: Joy in Him."[7]

It is what I desired for myself for this new year, for the rest of my life—to serve with joy. Literature Laureate Rabindranath Tagore said, "I slept and dreamt life was joy, I awoke and saw life was service, I acted and behold, service was joy."[8]

Questions at the Crossroads

I have always been a fan of Robert Frost. I especially love these lines at the end of his famous poem:

> Two roads diverged in a wood, and I—
> I took the one less traveled by,
> And that has made all the difference.[9]

Pause with me at the crossroads. Are these questions you have asked on your journey before?

- What if I took the wrong path? Will it still make a difference?
- What if I am in the wrong wood?
- What if none of it really matters, anyway?

I completed teaching through the book of Esther with my Sunday school class. Talk about being at the crossroads! Queen Esther was made "for such a time as this" (Esther 4:14). I wonder if she asked these questions:

---

7   Ann Voskamp, *One Thousand Gifts: A Dare to Live Fully Right Where You Are* (Grand Rapids: Zondervan, 2010), 197.
8   Rabindranath Tagore, "Rabindranath Tagore > Quotes > Quotable Quote," Goodreads, Accessed January 5, 2015, https://www.goodreads.com/quotes/15762-i-slept-and-dreamt-that-life-was-joy-i-awoke.
9   Robert Frost, "The Road Less Taken," Poetry Foundation, Accessed February 22, 2022, https://www.poetryfoundation.org/poems/44272/the-road-not-taken.

- What if I make the wrong decision?
- Will I die along with all of my people?
- What if I say the wrong thing at the wrong time?
- What if I let someone else lead the way?

Throughout life, we all find ourselves contemplating big life choices:

- Do I marry this guy or that one? What if I do not marry at all?
- What if I choose the wrong career path?
- What if I lose my job and do not have skills to choose another one?

I recently completed rereading the book *Bird by Bird* by Anne Lamott. It is a famous book for aspiring authors like me. Many of us writers think that if we just get a book deal and our words are published, that is all there is to life and we can rest content in our fame and fortune. Do not get me wrong. That would be amazing. We writers want to know that our words are making a difference; and if we are not changing the world, at least our words are changing one person. God is more concerned with our character in whatever career path we choose. He cares more that we are a person who reflects Him in all of life's doubts and joys. Anne's point is that even if a writer does make it through all the hoops to publishing, she will still be the same person on the other side of that milestone. The choice comes in how to handle success or struggles.[10]

None of us know what lies beyond the next turn in the path we have chosen. But we can know who travels with us. We can ask these questions when the path diverges:

---

10 Anne Lamott, *Bird by Bird: Some Instructions on Writing and Life* (New York: Anchor Books, 1994).

- What if the path ahead in my journey brings pain? How do I take the next step?
- What if I need to rest and get a better vision of the future?
- What if I let God direct my steps?

I have also always loved this wise saying from One Who can always make sense of the path ahead: "Trust in the Lord with all your heart, and do not lean on your own understanding. In all your ways acknowledge him, and he will make straight your paths" (Prov. 3:5-6).

The Fog Always Rises

I have a very deep theological issue to ponder: fog. One of my trips to Indonesia started out in a thick, soupy, foggy mess. Little did I know the trip would also end up messy. It would be messy in between, too. The fog was so thick, we could not see the toll booth as we drove past it. My son, Johnny III, was driving me to the Oklahoma City airport early that morning. We made it fine, thankfully. But it had its scary moments. I flew on to Denver and then San Francisco, where I met my co-worker and travel buddy.

When we arrived at the Singapore airport, the plot—or the fog—thickened. Right from the beginning, the trip was challenging for a variety of reasons. During the two-week trip, I felt that I was trapped under the fog of anger, doubt, and insecurity. I was so very thankful my friend/coworker/sister, Carrole, was with me. It took many months—maybe even years—to recover.

While I was at our national ministry partner's home in Sumatra, I received a message from my husband saying that our house had flooded. A pipe burst under the floor. He stated rather undramatically, "It won't be cleaned up when you get home." That was an understatement. It would be the beginning of a very long road of repairs and remodels to my home, which is also my workplace and my sanctuary. It would be under a fog of reconstruction for the next three months. Fog happens.

I have had other personal issues and situations that seemed like fog had descended again. It left me with a tired, soggy, foggy brain. I was filled with doubt and confusion, teetering on the edge of depression. During this part of my life journey, I found a book in which the author writes in the first chapters that the fog always rises.[11] Sometimes, it looks like the sun is never going to peek through the heavy coating of the low-lying clouds again. But it does. One Scripture that shines brightly is Psalm 119:105: "Your word is a lamp to my feet and a light to my path"—or in this case, my foggy path. He gives us light just enough for us to see the next steps. He gives us His Word, Himself, His Presence, friends, peace.

I searched in Scripture for the word "fog." Here is what I found: "For now we see in a mirror dimly, but then face to face. Now I know in part; then I shall know fully, even as I have been fully known" (1 Cor. 13:12). The unseen is then clearly revealed.

Of course, we will not know fully until we are together with Him forever in Heaven. We learn lessons along the way. For instance:

- I learned that the pain of remodeling is always rewarded with beauty and comfort for years to come.
- I learned that in my present struggles, He uses my doubts to help me depend more fully on Him.
- I learned that He uses my questions to seek help and to seek Him more diligently.

His presence peeks through like rays of light piercing the thick fog. He is always there. He just had a veiled face. The light comes because the fog always rises.

---

[11] Tammie Pittsley, Ed.D., *Rising Above the Fog: A Christian's Guide to Habits for Healing Depression* (Independently published, 2018), 1.

Occupation: Bridge Builder

Left or Right, liberal or conservative, pro-choice or pro-life, optimist or pessimist, extrovert or introvert—on and on the list goes. We are known by our labels. We know others by the labels we give them. We like to fit people in our boxes so that we know how to interact with them, but there seems to be no room for boxes in the middle. No centrists allowed.

There are also these labels: non-believers or believers. Our calling as believers, or followers of Jesus, is not to stay firmly on the right. It is not to never cross over, to never know another world, to never see unseen people. Our calling is to follow Jesus to the other side. Jesus did that with Zacchaeus, with the woman at the well, and with the leper.

Please do not misinterpret—there are some non-negotiable beliefs that we stake our lives on. But this is not an "us" and "them" world. We are called to be bridge-builders. I have served in that role before in my previous work as a missions minister. I linked church members with serving opportunities around the world. I brought challenges to members to see beyond themselves and connect to a larger picture. With my work in Indonesia, I served as the official bridge-builder between that country and our nonprofit home office. I served as a voice for abused and enslaved women and girls so that people at home could know more about their world and how to provide freedom and how to develop eyes to focus on unseen people and their needs. I have done that in my work as director of communications—telling the stories and showing the needs of all the women and girls served in the hardest places, with the purpose of bringing safety and freedom through providing awareness and ways to support the work.

My ultimate role as a bridge-builder is to live like Christ in our disconnected, chaotic world—to bring His light to *all* the people in *all* the boxes with *all* the labels. I do that through my attitudes and actions every day. I invite them to experience life on the other side. My job as a bridge-builder is to let them know they are very much loved in whatever box they are in with whatever label is applied. God sees them and loves them, just the way they are, and invites them to cross the bridge to enjoy the new life He has to offer. That is my calling as a bridge-builder. That is your calling, too. Wherever we find ourselves, we know who we are and what our job description is.

And God Said

It was a whisper. I had heard His whisper before. In the night when I woke up, I heard it. I had been troubled that week. I mean, I have never had to help write global communications for a nonprofit during a pandemic. We all found ourselves in strange settings during those days. Parents suddenly morphed into homeschool teachers. Employees found themselves working from home. Pastors were preaching to empty sanctuaries and video cameras. It was weird for all of us.

I already worked from home, so that was not a big deal, except that Johnny started working from home, too. I gave him my nice, quiet, dedicated office space; and I began working in the sitting room in the front of the house. I labeled it my "writing den" during that season. I was not suffering very much. On nice days, I worked out on the deck when I was not on a Zoom call (which seemed to be very often). My days were different when I began sharing my quiet home all day long with Johnny. We developed a rhythm, and it worked out. We had not had lunch together on weekdays that often in a very long time.

Our neighborhood was much the same, except that when I was out for my walk, I saw neighbors talking with one another from a minimum of six feet apart. The kids were out making noise and running amok every day, all day like it was summer vacation.

Back to the Voice in the night, I went to sleep thinking about how everything had changed. Life was topsy-turvy the world over.

Then God said, "I am the same. I never change."

I replied, "So what am I supposed to do now, God, while the world is constantly changing?"

He spoke again, and I felt Him say, "Just keep doing what you are doing. Keep writing the stories. Do it for the precious enslaved and abused women and girls. Do it for Me."

It reminded me of the Scripture I selected as my theme verse for our recent She Is Safe annual meeting: "And he who was seated on the throne said, 'Behold, I am making all things new.' Also he said, 'Write this down, for these words are trustworthy and true'" (Rev. 21:5). Write the words that are trustworthy and true. Yes, that was my calling. That is what I desired to do—a calling confirmed even in uncertain times. That was all I heard. I quickly went back to sleep.

No, it was not an audible thundering Voice. As I said, it was an inaudible whisper. But it was very clear to me—God said just keep doing what you are doing, even in unprecedented situations, even when social distancing is a thing; when you have to do church virtually; when you see grocery store shelves empty of toilet paper. Just keep doing what you are doing because when everything changes, He does not.

5
Seeing and Meeting Unseen People in My Neighborhood

I READ HIS OBITUARY IN the newspaper one morning; my next-door neighbor, Mike, had passed away. He was the owner of yappy dogs and a red SUV and quick with kind words and a smile. I would miss him—not that we ever talked very much, aside from just a few greetings across the property line as we were rolling our trash carts to the street or getting in or out of our cars on our parallel driveways. He would ask about my granddaughter. He would tell me he was off traveling somewhere with his work and ask if I would please watch out for unusual activity at his home while he was away. It was just neighbor stuff—nothing big or important.

I remember with a smile the experience recently by our shared backyard fence. My big yellow Lab, Daisy, was going berserk with her big dog bark. As I was scolding her from our deck for her loud interruptions, I heard a voice. "Hello? Hi! Hello!"

I walked to the fence. "Hello?" I answered.

Mike said with a smile in his voice, "It's okay. She is barking at my new puppy. They just need to get to know each other." With that introduction, he swooped up his little, yappy puppy and held her up high over the fence so I could get a good look at her.

"What a cute dog. I know you'll enjoy her."

"I will. So don't worry about your dogs barking. It's fine."

I am glad Mike had some companionship. I knew he was divorced, and his grown and married kids and grandkids did not live nearby.

A few weeks later, Mike and I met near our cars again. This time, he had a rental car that he was packing. He walked over to chat with me. I asked how he had been doing.

"Well, I've been sick. I've lost vision in my eye and had to have surgery." He had dark glasses on, so I could not see the damage. "In fact, I'm headed back to the hospital in Oklahoma City for another surgery."

I expressed my apologies for not knowing he was sick. That was the last time I spoke with him. He did not return, and my husband and I wondered what was happening to him. Then I read the obituary.

That summer, I stood outside talking with my neighbor lady on the other side of our property. She told me her husband was now in the veterans' hospital nearby, and her daughter drove her there often to visit with him. I knew he had Parkinson's disease. He was not going to get better. I did not know the level of her sadness until I saw it close up in her eyes. You cannot see pain from a distance driving by on the way to your garage or walking by the house on a daily walk with a wave and a "How are you?"

On a normal day in October several years ago, only three houses down on my calm, tree-lined street, a brutal murder happened—crime tape, news crews, and helicopter flyovers. A college-aged son shot his family in cold blood. I had no clue the depth of anger that was brewing in that house the million-and-one times I had walked by it on my daily exercise routine. I did not even know the family. It was only three doors down.

It all made me wonder. As I walked by these houses in my nice, "safe" neighborhood, I did not have any idea what was happening beyond their front doors and welcome mats. I usually had my music blaring in my ears so I could keep up my walking pace. I was thinking about my "to-do" list or something else related to me. Sometimes, just sometimes, I prayed as I walked. Usually, it was for me, my family, and friends, or things related to each of those areas.

I know I cannot see all the unseen pain and problems brewing beyond each closed garage door. But I can pray for my neighbors that they will find peace and joy in their everyday problems and the courage to seek help when the pain is too much. I can do that. I am challenged to at least once a week, while on my walk through the neighborhood, to pray for my neighbors. Will you join me in praying for yours?

Do You See Them?

Tell me the name of the person who last bagged your groceries. How about the person at the gas station who gave you your fountain drink? At the restaurant where you last dined, what was the name of your server? Here are the ones I remember: Juan, John, Julie. I only know those names because I have been trying to pay more attention lately. (It was a coincidence they all started with a *J*, but it did help me remember them!)

Juan is the guy at my local grocery store who sometimes bags my groceries. Sometimes, I go to the store and bag my own; but honestly, I like it better when someone does it for me. Juan is an easy guy to remember because he is a talker. As he bagged, he was talking. As he walked with me to my car and put my groceries in, he was talking. The topics covered everything from the hundred-degree weather, to making sure his kids had a good work ethic, to what he was doing to celebrate an upcoming holiday. Juan did not have a name tag on; but when he helped me put a propane tank into my car, I thanked him and asked him his name. He smiled and shook my hand. Next time I go to that store, I will look for him, call him by name, and expect a big smile.

On the way home from the store, I stopped at the drive-through window at the gas station where I liked to purchase fountain drinks. I got a couple of thirty-two-ounce drinks—a diet Dr. Pepper for Johnny and a Coke Zero with vanilla for me. The young man who gave me my drinks to order at the window that day was named John. I looked at his nametag. "Thanks, John. I appreciate your help." He gave a big smile. I hoped he would be there the next time I was thirsty for my special-order drink.

About twice a month, my discipleship group meets at a local restaurant. We are often served by the same people week after week. One time, one of the women surprised me. I ordered ice water while I waited for the other two women to arrive. She brought it with a slice of lemon.

"You remembered I like lemon in my drink? That's amazing." It had been several weeks since she had been our server. "Thank you, Julie."

She smiled. Thankfully, she had a nametag on. Later that morning, after the girls left, Julie approached me and asked me to please pray for her teenage daughter, who was experiencing some special challenges. "I watch your group and love what you do every time—Bible study and prayer. Thank you for praying for us." Julie went on to describe her struggles as a single mom and her desire to attend church, but she always had to work on Sunday mornings. I wrote her request in my Bible study journal, so I would not forget.

I usually do not remember things very well. Johnny and I can watch a movie he knows we have seen, but I think we are watching it for the first time. I do not recall names well either, unless I am paying close attention. Then I write the names down quickly before I forget and try to remember to pray for them that week.

That is my encouragement to you, too. Pay attention. Look people in the eyes and listen. Ask their name and use it in your conversation with them. Try to frequent the same places to see if you can see those same people often. That is how you start to build relationships. That is how the unseen become seen. Start with a name.

You Are Welcome Here.

"Welcome! Won't you come in and stay awhile?"

We all want to feel welcomed and comfortable in someone else's home. Yet hospitality is an uncomfortable word for many of us. (I mean, it literally has the word *hospital* in it. Nobody wants that.) Unless God has gifted you with a natural, outgoing, welcoming spirit, where whipping up a five-course meal or serving homemade cookies warm from the oven is easy for you, then you understand what I mean. We think our homes have to be spotless; our appetizers should belong on the cover of a magazine; and we do not look like we have been running around like a crazy woman sweating, cleaning, cooking, and doing laundry all day. Honestly, while we want to have an appealing presence and a well-ordered household, that is not what is important. It is you, your home, and us there together in it.

When I think of hospitality, I immediately think of my mother. She was always the quintessential genteel Southern hostess. Mama loved to decorate for all the holidays. She loved it when her family was all together in one room, preferably seated around the dinner table. She was the perfect pastor's wife—a helpmate to her husband, standing by his side with a smile. Mama loved to bake chocolate chip cookies and deliver them to new neighbors, families in need, or us when we came home to visit. (I do not think she would be very impressed with my slice 'n bake skills.) My mother embodied hospitality.

When I think of hospitality, I think of visiting in the humble home of a new friend in northeastern Bangladesh. Although he was obviously living on a poor man's wage, he embodied Asian hospitality when he walked to the village market and purchased a bottle of soda for us to drink. He knew we could not drink his water but wanted to offer us his best. I wanted to tell him, "No, please, don't spend your hard-earned money on us." But that would have been dishonoring him and his home; so we graciously smiled, thanked him, sat on the mat on his floor, and sipped our soda out of plastic cups.

When I think of hospitality, I think of the sweet Mexican grandmother who cooked our entire mission team homemade flour tortillas. She served them hot out of her oven with a big toothy smile. And we all gathered in a circle to thank God for our meal.

When I think of hospitality, I think of sitting in the home of a young mother in Sumatra, Indonesia. Through the many trips I took there, I visited many homes and the experience was always similar and sweet. We sat shoeless on the floor in a big circle on brightly colored plastic mats. My travel mates and I were always the center of attention and were served first—big mounds of white rice, fresh vegetables, and usually small portions of fish or chicken. And we always enjoyed strong Sumatran coffee.

I was welcomed. I felt at home, even when I was so far away from my home. If they could speak English, they would usher us in and say, "Come on in! You are welcome here."

As I think of those humble homes, I know our homes do not have to be magazine quality to host someone for dinner. We do not have to serve gourmet meals. Pizza or sandwiches and chips will be just fine or a bottle of soda or a cup of strong coffee. All we need is to invite someone and say when they arrive, "Come on in! You are welcome here."

The Sky Is Falling

Yes, we hear you Chicken Little. The sky is indeed falling, one acorn at a time, right on top of your tiny, little head. I always loved this story I remember from my childhood. I liked to say the characters' names—Goosey Loosey, Foxy Loxy, Henny Penny, Ducky Lucky, and Turkey Lurkey. They are just fun to repeat and make me smile.

The sky really is not falling, of course; but sometimes, it feels like it. It feels like it when:

- So many people you know and love lose their oil-patch-related jobs.
- You go for a walk in your neighborhood and see eleven "For Sale" signs posted in yards of homes all around you.
- A presidential election is coming, and you have to consider whether to vote or not to vote or to choose the lesser of two evils.

- A good friend tells you she has cancer and shares with you the aggressive treatment plan including radiation, chemo, and surgery.
- Leaders in countries around the world act like children and vote to take their toys and go home, regardless of how it affects people and the rest of the world.
- My sweet, goofy, lovable Lab, Daisy, has to have surgery on her leg again—her third surgery.

All of that happened in one week. It makes you wonder. Who is in control of this nutty mess? Is it greedy oil company executives? Politicians hungry for power? Individual mindless choices? Yes, all of the above. We are all to blame for choices made, and we all can choose how we respond—with anger, avoidance, tears, or cynicism. I have chosen all those coping mechanisms. None of them work.

As I was taking a morning walk one day in my neighborhood, I noticed all the "For Sale" signs that had popped up out of the ground, along with all the political signs. As I walked, I listened to the songs blaring in my ears from my playlist. Those songs were selected because they have a fast beat and were supposed to make me walk quicker and sweat more. And they did. But I also noticed titles of songs I had chosen carried a similar message: "There's Hope in Front of Me," "Hope Can Change Everything," "Pushing Back the Dark," and "Glow in the Dark."

Hope, a light in the dark—I am reminded, even when the sky feels like it is falling, God is still with us. It is still our purpose as followers of Jesus to shine His light in a dark world. Then I realized I have meaningful, purposeful work to do each day. My husband provided well for us in his oil-related engineering work.

I received a text message from my daughter as I continued my walk. She told me about the daily adventures of my two-year-old granddaughter and about how active our soon-to-be-born second granddaughter was that day. Another message followed from my friend with the cancer diagnosis about how grateful she was for so many people supporting her and praying for her.

As I finished my walk and headed toward home, I was sharply aware that there was not a "For Sale" sign in front of my house.

I will still read the grim headlines later on my news apps about the domino effects of plummeting oil prices and European countries trying to survive. When I opened my front door, there was my broken dog who limps and thumps her tail and lets me know she is okay, and it is going to be okay—not perfect and not without challenges, but all is well today.

No, Chicken Little, the sky is not falling—not today. It is going to be okay because there is always hope and we get to share it with one another.

The Race of a Lifetime

The streetlights flickered on. The runners leaned in toward the starting line, and then . . . They were off. Some were running, some walking, all sweating in the late July muggy night. A hundred racers, from ten-year-old boys to a seventy-four-year-old woman, with numbers pinned to their shirts, a race toward the darkness. The deepening darkness, representing the oppression and fear that women and girls face every day, was pierced with hope—from flashlights, reflectors and prayers. Most of these runners would finish the race in a short time; return to their cool and comfortable homes; and sleep soundly without the fear of hunger, violence, and disease. They would never meet any of the unseen thousands of women their registration fee would help. They would never see them in person, since they lived literally half-a-world away from Oklahoma; but the need of abused and trafficked women and girls in Southeast Asia was a glaring evil. These Southwestern Americans could do something to help. So they ran with enthusiasm, with determination, and with hope.

I snapped their photo as the racers lunged forward on their journey at our community hospital. It was appropriate that they would start at our beautiful, modern medical complex. The runners were supporting the work of She Is Safe. We knew the importance of a healthy balance of body, mind, and spirit for each woman and girl we envisioned to help. The hospital represented physical health. I thought of the women I had met during my last visit to Central Indonesia. I remembered sitting at a table with mothers and their children in their laps, all of them HIV-positive. I listened to them tell what they were thankful for and requested prayers that their children would be safe from physical abuse and safe from human traffickers. A few days after that, I was in a village in Sumatra sitting on the floor in the humble home of a young mother.

I smiled as they told me about the health benefits of bananas. She said, "You eat the banana for health, and then"—she touched her beautiful brown face—"you rub the peel on your face for soft skin." I am quite sure the dermatologist in our area had not prescribed that ointment lately.

Halfway through the race, the runners circled the middle school. There, the runners were offered cups of clean, cold water and shouts of encouragement from volunteers. Representing education, the school reminded me of the many little girls throughout Asia, Africa, and the Middle East who would only receive the very basic levels of education, if any at all. Their mothers did not have money for their school fees. They had only enough money to spare for their brothers to go to school.

More volunteers flashed lights to direct runners to the next turn. In the next few minutes, they would head back to the hospital and the finish line. Every racer who started the race finished the race, just as every woman I prayed for in those circles on the floor in Indonesia would one day face the end of life. I prayed for these women to have a healthy spiritual life, to not live in fear of a god they could never please. I prayed for them to know the true God of love, care, and compassion. I prayed for them all to know Him. I prayed that I could make Him known to all.

The race was over. The winners were declared, and medals were awarded. Awareness was raised and funds donated. But the race of a lifetime continues—a race to the darkness to bring light, health, and hope.

I Had No Idea

Sitting there in my cozy room looking out the front window onto the real world outside, I was reminded that I did not have to travel far from home to know everyone had issues in life they were battling. They were fighting problems that we had no idea about until our paths crossed and we stopped to listen.

Recently my next-door neighbor came to my door to tell me about some problems with the trees that we had along our shared property line. This is a sweet lady I interacted with infrequently. We waved to each other as we passed each other's driveways or shouted out a good morning as we walked to our mailboxes. We each had our own lives and probably would never have known each other if our houses were not just a few short feet apart. Regardless, we were decent neighbors and cared about each other—but, usually, from a comfortable distance.

On this particular evening, as she stood in my doorway to tell me about what was causing some distress to our blackjack oak trees, I shared with her about my husband's recent back injury. She had no idea. Then she began to tell me about her husband, who had Parkinson's disease and had now developed dementia. I did not know about the dementia. She fought back tears as she told me about the man she loved and had been married to for sixty years, who now had no idea who she was. Every day, she drove thirty miles to the veterans' home to visit him; and every day, he did not know her name. I had no words for her except that I was very sorry and I could not imagine how hard that was for her every day. I would never have known of her daily emptiness and loneliness if our little oak trees were not dying and shedding leaves in the middle of August.

It reminded me of that saying, "Be nice to everyone because you never know who is having a bad day." I think that is a saying. If it is not, it should be.

A few days after that brief encounter with my neighbor, a new friend invited me to meet for a visit at a fast-food restaurant, drink a soda, and share a few minutes of life together. She asked me to talk first as she listened, sipping her drink, while I spouted off all the "exciting" adventures of my life story. Very kindly, she listened, asked questions, and genuinely took time to know me. Then, it was her turn. I had no idea. She was in the process of recovering from cancer. I listened as I tried to understand the pain, the process, and the journey she and her family were still on.

Everybody has a story. Everybody has a pain they are carrying that we can help carry if we stop and listen. Getting involved in people's lives can get messy and time-consuming—and be absolutely, totally worth it.

Who Is Behind That Door?

I was out for my morning walk. As was my recent custom, I walked without any earbuds stuck in my head. I wanted no distractions in order to leave margin for my brain to decompress. I wanted to enjoy the moment and the red and green Christmas decorations that had overtaken the orange and brown pumpkins and leaves.

As I passed by one house on a corner, my brain did what it does when it relaxes—it fills up again. I remembered the family who had lived there many years ago. Back when my children were in grade school, they went to church and school with the little girl and boy who lived there. They were a happy family—or so it seemed on the outside, for a while.

Trouble brewed behind those doors—discontent. A husband who traveled with his company developed wandering eyes. He found satisfaction in another country, in the arms of another woman. Divorce begins with discontent.

Those beautiful children grew into adults who made choices. The girl moved to Los Angeles to pursue a passion for movie-making. She succeeded, and that same passion chose a same-sex relationship. The boy grew up, and he and his girlfriend went a step too far. A beautiful baby boy with special needs was born. Choices breed consequences.

As I made more steps toward home, I passed by the home where, years ago, a disgruntled, divorced man took out his frustration on the husband of his ex-wife. His rage found expression through gunfire.

I finished my walk in front of my home. What happens behind that door? It was not infidelity nor gunfire. Sometimes, there was anger. Often, there was selfishness, greed, and idolatry. But also behind those doors, I met God each morning. I read in the pages of God's Word Who He is—King, Author, Counselor, Prince of Peace, the God Who helps me with my fears, anxieties, and discontent.

How to Celebrate Your Birthday Week

I have always been the baby. I was the third and last child in my family growing up; therefore, I was the baby. And I was treated that way. It was fine with me. My Southern mama knew how to spoil me and keep me close (until I grew up and became way too independent.)

Then, somehow, in some of my groups of friends, I was suddenly the oldest. How did that happen? Age has a way of creeping up on you and taking you by surprise, along with the gray hair and all the other things that happen to a "woman of a certain age"—whatever age that is. So, a few years ago, when I turned sixty, I decided to designate it my birthday week, not just a day. It seemed like a momentous occasion; so I thought, why not celebrate all week? If there is no stopping the turning of the calendar pages, why not embrace it? It seems a bit indulgent. I know. That is okay.

In the last year, death has come way too early for too many people I know--at least, in my opinion. A few women near my age had died, including one to an aneurysm and one in a car crash due to a heart attack. A doctor, father, and husband in his forties was alive and living a good life with his family; and the next day, he was gone. I do not want to depress you, but my point is to celebrate life while you can. Why not have a birthday week?

For me, that included a trip to the zoo with my four grandchildren. I got to feed a giraffe and see a baby elephant. It was a good day with lots of sweat, steps, and smiles from giggly girls and a jabbering baby boy. My week included time swaying in my hammock, sitting on my deck listening to the birds as the sun came up, and doing lots of reading in both of those locations. I took a long walk on trails nearby. It felt good. My week also included indulging in a cold brew latte and a coffee-flavored brownie ball in a local coffee shop, all by myself. The introvert in me enjoyed the quiet, the solitude, and the time to do absolutely nothing—just being still. That felt good, too.

God holds all time in His hands—whether it is packed with deadlines and meetings and an endless "to-do" list or walking my dog down my street shaded by draping oak trees. My challenge to you is not only to seize the day but also seize the week. We do not know how much time we have on this earth. When it is over, as the apostle Paul said, "For to me to live is Christ, and to die is gain" (Phil. 1:21). Start planning your birthday week now and schedule a time to celebrate. At the same time, take time to pause and see things and people you have overlooked.

6
Seeing the Underserved in a Nation of Plenty

TO THIS DAY, I STILL call her "Group"—my summer missions partner in the Maryland/D.C. area. I turned nineteen while I was there. I took my first airplane trip, alone, that summer. I opened an envelope from a church member on that flight that had fifty dollars in it. I will always remember that moment thinking, *This trip is bigger than me.* Little did I know, that trip would change my life.

Jennifer, from Missouri, was "much" older by three years. She was a college senior, and I was a freshman. We started as strangers and ended as lifelong friends. We knocked on a lot of doors. I had never seen so many doors lined up together in the cities surrounding D.C. We knocked on each one and asked the people if they went to church. We scribbled down their answers and left a flyer about an upcoming children's event to be held in their local park.

On our days off, we went to D.C. and experienced the sights—the Smithsonian museums, the Capitol, Ford's Theatre, and the FBI Headquarters. It was on these adventures that we stood waiting for the bus to come and take us to the next sight. The driver would announce on his microphone, "Keep your groups together as you board the bus." Jennifer and I looked at each other. We were our own group. That is the way it was for twelve weeks that summer.

One of the main experiences that stuck with me was when one of the pastors we worked with for a few weeks drove us through the area. "Just look at all the people!" I will never forget the row after row after row of apartments and houses that all looked the same. When that twelve-week experience was over, I felt like Group and I knocked on all those doors and did backyard Bible clubs with all those children. But God began to do something in my heart. This was personal. My job was to share that personal love with people to whom God led me. It was a lifelong, life-changing task that was indeed bigger than me.

Tony with a "T"

Two church vans full of teenagers, supplies, and my little family headed west from Oklahoma to New Mexico. That probably did not sound like a huge trek, but it was when your van was full of the above-mentioned items. In addition to the van full of teenagers, there were a trailer full of supplies to conduct a Vacation Bible School at the Baptist Center in inner-city Albuquerque, my three-year-old son and five-year-old daughter and lots of their toys, plus luggage for all the above teenagers and our family and food and cooking supplies for one week. We were going prepared. We had daily lesson plans ready to implement complete with games, crafts, and Bible stories.

As prepared as we were, we had no idea that the week would bring gunshots, a child locked in a room, and the death of the parent of one of the children at our Bible school. I remember the little girls from the neighborhood that week were fascinated with my daughter's hair. Rachel—my blonde, blue-eyed little girl, was smiling and standing in the middle of children mostly of various shades of brown and all with dark hair and eyes.. She was loving every minute.

At registration at the beginning of the week, a six-year-old boy stepped up to the table to get his nametag. "What's your name?" one of our teenage workers asked.

The boy replied boldly, "My name is Tony. Tony with a *T*."

I'm not sure how else you would spell that name, but I will never forget that little boy and the challenges he gave us that week.

I also have cemented in my memory the little boy connected with the gunshot we heard that week. One night, as we tried to sleep on blow-up mattresses and sleeping bags in the Baptist Center, the night crackled with the unmistakable blast of gunfire. It originated only a few blocks from our building. Manuel was a Hispanic five-year-old who had been attending the Bible club that week. His father had been caught in a drug deal that ended badly. Manuel's dad died that night.

The next day, Manuel came to our group; but this time, he locked himself in one of the Center's rooms. It took over an hour and a lot of conversation to get him to unlock the door. I wonder what happened to Manuel in the years after we were there. I hope he chose the ways offered by the Baptist Center and modeled the men who ran the programs there and demonstrated the love of Christ.

As we prepared to leave on Friday, the neighborhood children did not want us to leave. One of the high school football players with our group, a rather large gentle giant, tried to make his way to the van with children hanging off every limb and one on his back. I am not sure who was smiling more—him or the children.

I smile as I remember Tony with a *T* and all the children of inner-city Albuquerque. I hope they remember two van loads of loud teenagers, blond-haired children and a few adults who tried to display the love of Jesus. I pray that they felt seen, treasured and loved.

On July 5, in the Dark, in Dupont Circle, D.C.

Do you remember where you were on July 5, 1979? I know many of you were not born yet, and others were too young to remember. After all, that was many years ago. I was nineteen years old and a summer missionary in Montgomery County, Maryland. It was my first time experiencing something so spectacular.

My summer missions partner, Jennifer, ("Group"), decided we wanted to go down to see the fireworks from the vantage point of the National Mall. The display had been delayed from the fourth due to rain.

We had taken public transportation several times on our days off from our locations in Maryland into downtown D.C. Our days had been full of Vacation Bible School, door-to-door surveys, and a variety of other tasks our ministry leaders had for us to do. On our given day off, we ventured down to see the sights. Jennifer chose a location (like the FBI building); and I would choose Ford's Theatre, the Capitol, or the White House the next time—and always a museum (such as the National Museum of Natural History or the National Air and Space Museum). We had a great time. We were young and inexperienced, and everything was fresh and new to us.

So why not go see the fireworks? Why not go into a mob of thousands of people on a national holiday? The brand-new metro (the subway) was being debuted with free rides that day. We decided to take the bus like we usually did and then take the free subway ride back to Rockville.

We got off the bus at Dupont Circle, walked to the Mall, and found our place on the ground to enjoy the show. It was dazzling. Never had a country Arkansas girl ever experienced anything like it. *Oohs* and *aahs* rippled all around us. Then, as the last blasts fizzled, it was over; and all that humanity started to ooze toward the Mall metro entrance. We realized quickly we were in big trouble—too many people and not enough opportunities to board a train.

We decided to walk back to Dupont Circle and find our bus. It was easy breezy—until it was not. We waited an hour for our bus. It was very dark and, I am sure, dangerous for two naive young women. Jennifer had just finished her senior year, and I was only a freshman. She was much older and wiser than I.

I said, "Just get me out of here."

As we were contemplating what to do next, a drunk man staggered by us at the bus stop and said, "It's not safe for you girls out here."

Jennifer found a pay phone (there were no cell phones invented yet) and called our host family. He graciously drove the distance in the late hours to retrieve us. We were humbled and humiliated but safe once again.

I learned other lessons that summer. It is okay to work with children all summer, even when that is not your giftedness. It is okay to be homesick; you eventually get over it. It is good to be dependent on others; but mostly, it is important to realize that our ultimate dependence is on God—on July 5, in the dark, in Dupont Circle, D.C.

Journey to Freedom

I am a child of the American South—specifically, the states of Arkansas, Tennessee, and Alabama. I did not move from the South until I was a college graduate at age twenty-one. Then I moved all the way to the Southwest to Texas and then Oklahoma. I was only a little girl when I lived in northern Alabama—six and seven years old in 1966 and 1967. I do not remember very much of those days, except that I was in the first grade, my teacher's name was Mrs. Glaze, I liked Batman, and my daddy pastored a Baptist church there with a cemetery that had creepy graves in the back. My childhood was happy; and my brother and sister and I were loved, cared for, and protected.

I have no memory of the racial tensions in that state that were sparked in 1965 further south in the small city of Selma. I do not ever remember my parents telling us there were any differences in people. On the contrary, I remember listening to my mother speak in women's missions meetings about how much God loves all people and how we need to share that love. I remember similar words as my dad spoke from the pulpit the famous words of John 3:16: that God loved the world, everyone in the world, so very much that He gave His only beloved Son.

That is why when I grew older, I could not understand why there was such anger between white and black people. I did not understand why our church people were so eager to give to mission causes throughout the continent of

Africa but spoke in such disrespectful terms about black people from the American South. Location was the only difference I could determine.

Through the years, I have learned much about cultures and the way culture shapes people. I have grown to see how fear and power and control cause wars and death and limit freedom and the basic rights of humanity. Perhaps, that is why I made sure my children were exposed to different cultures and people to help them understand that God made all people equally. All are of value. All are important.

I have studied the history of the abolition movement led by William Wilberforce in England in the 1800s. I have lived near a major Civil War battleground, Shiloh, in western Tennessee. I have studied the leadership of President Abraham Lincoln. Perhaps, all of that led me to be involved through She Is Safe as a part of the modern freedom movement to prevent, rescue, and restore women and girls trapped in abuse and human trafficking.

A few years ago, I sat in a movie theater watching the movie, *Selma*. The room was filled with black people from my community who were proud of their history. Together, we experienced pride in watching leaders stand for values and the very basic right to vote. I felt with them the anger of not being heard or seen and being treated with disrespect merely based on color. History is replete with rights and wrongs done on both sides of the civil rights movement. Clearly, fifty years after those events occurred, there is still hate, tension, and unrest. Hate and fear do not easily loosen their grip.

"Freedom" is a lofty word we normally take for granted. But I know those who do not, such as the Coloured people group of the Northern Cape province in South Africa I met and served with years ago, the little girls in Indonesia who were brutally raped and rescued by loving and kind women with whom we worked, a young woman on a southeast Asian island who was HIV-positive but was rescued from a life of prostitution.

It seems to me that people who name the name of Christ should be the first ones to speak up for freedom for all people—regardless of skin color, regardless of location—because we know the truth. "'You will know the truth, and the truth will set you free'" (John 8:32).

So today, choose to see people from all backgrounds. Celebrate freedom. Share the truth. Demonstrate love.

Michigan, D.C., Chocolate Milk, and Puppets

Our church bus was loaded with seventeen people from south Arkansas. Most of them were teenagers. We were lumbering north toward Flint, Michigan, for a week of inner-city mission work with children. You would think the teenagers would know some basic geography, especially about the United States. And yet this question came from the back of the bus: "Do we get to see the Grand Canyon on the way?"

This was the same teenage girl who was confused when asked if chocolate milk comes from brown cows—the same one who, on a mission trip the following year in Washington D.C., stuck her head out of the bus window, looked upward and said, "What's that tall thing?" It was the Washington Monument. It was the same girl who had never traveled out of her cozy cocoon of family and friends who, with her thick southern drawl, could smile in every situation, effortlessly lead children in games and activities, and set up a puppet stage with a show ready in only a few minutes.

I am not sure she traveled again outside the state once our youth ministry mission trip days were over. But in those few years, her boundaries were broadened to see a bigger picture. She saw people in her own nation. She was willing to go, yet not to see the Grand Canyon but to see the "tall thing" in D.C. There, she met people from all over the world. She heard accents and languages from people that left her puzzled yet still smiling at the wonder of it all. And then she was happily content to go back to her cocooned living. There is nothing wrong with that. But I am pretty sure she never got her passport.

A New York Experience

I have experienced New York before—three times in New York City. I have experienced Times Square and the Statue of Liberty and subways and taxis. I have even walked in neighborhoods in Brooklyn and Queens and enjoyed the New York City multicultural experience. But I had not experienced upstate New York until this adventure, and it was definitely a unique and beautiful trip.

My mentor/friend/coworker Cherylann invited me to join her to connect with a church that had been an ongoing supporter of She Is Safe and specifically for the work in Indonesia. The week was full of activity: nine different speaking opportunities, meeting lots of great people, manning our She Is Safe booth, sharing with everyone from first-graders to senior adults about She Is Safe and how they could be involved. It was good stuff.

I spent most of my time continuing to watch and learn from Cherylann, giving out resources from our booth at the church, and leading in a few of the teaching venues. At a Christian school, I told the Eastern parable of the monkey and the fish. This is one of my favorite stories that helps us see how sometimes trying to help people can end up hurting them if you do not take time to understand the needs and cultural context of the people you are serving. Read and enjoy and then consider the consequences of actions:

> A typhoon had temporarily stranded a monkey on an island. In a secure, protected place, while waiting for the raging waters to recede, he spotted a fish swimming against the current. It seemed obvious to the monkey that the fish was struggling and in need of assistance. Being of kind heart, the monkey resolved to help the fish.
>
> A tree precariously dangled over the very spot where the fish seemed to be struggling. At considerable risk to himself, the monkey moved far out on a limb, reached down and snatched the fish from the threatening waters. Immediately scurrying back to the safety of his shelter, he carefully laid the fish on

dry ground. For a few moments, the fish showed excitement, but soon settled into a peaceful rest. Joy and satisfaction swelled inside the monkey. He had successfully helped another creature.[12]

Think about it:

- What was the monkey's motivation?
- What words would you use to describe the monkey as he went out over the raging water on a precarious limb to "help" the fish?
- Why did the monkey "help" the fish by taking it out of the water?
- What did the monkey assume about fish "culture"?
- How do you think the fish felt about the "help" it received?
- What advice would you give the monkey for future situations in which he would like to help?

This is one of my favorite stories because it is about culture and those who are different from us—not wrong, just different. It always makes me wonder, how many fights would not happen, or wars begin, or hurtful words and gestures cease if we took time to understand those who are different from us? What would happen if we got to know them, to see them; to know them not as a category or a religion or a race or even a culture but as a person—a precious person God made, and knows, and loves, and gave His Son for? If we did, innocent people would still be alive; prejudice would not be an explosive issue; and friendships would be forged across barriers that seem formidable now.

What would have happened if only the monkey cared so much about the fish that he would meet the needs of the fish in the way the fish needed, not in the only way the monkey knew? Was the monkey uncaring? No. Was he insensitive? Yes, because he could not see past his own way of doing things. He thought everyone should be like him, and he came to rescue them from

---

12 Duane Elmer, *Cross Cultural Connections: Stepping Out and Fitting in Around the World* (Downers Grove: InterVarsity Press, 2002), 14

themselves. Maybe not everyone needs rescuing. Maybe everyone just needs a friend just to be seen for who they are.

Most of the time during my week in New York, I just tried to connect with people, listening and learning. That was the blessing I liked the most. I loved meeting people who unselfishly gave of their time and resources to help people like me they had never met but shared a common desire to serve God through helping women and girls in hard-to-reach places. These were people who spent their days promoting free trade organizations; who had adopted children—some of whom had provided many challenges; who opened their homes and stocked the pantry for guests to enjoy, including amazing women who shared their husbands with the United States military and a family who answered the phone at 4:30 a.m. to pull a rental car out of the mud.

I enjoyed unexpected beauty in upstate New York. It was the dead of winter, but there was still beauty. Far from the glitz and glamor of Broadway, I found a deep black sky studded with sparkling diamond stars. Our host home was far out of town in the country, which offered us a quiet refuge, as well as a glorious night sky whenever we took a moment to look up; take a deep, frosty breath; and enjoy the view. We also took a few hours one afternoon and drove up to Vermont. It was a new state for me to experience. I wondered what the trees on the hills would look like if it were autumn; but regardless, it was quaint and old and full of antique stores and frozen ponds.

I should have known the week would have its challenges when it started off with antibiotics as I recovered from a sinus infection. Then, the eighty-mile drive to the airport in the dark was thick with freezing fog. All was great until later in the week when I woke up at 3:00 a.m. with a stomach bug. I will spare you the details, but it was not pretty. It zapped me of energy and my desire to live that day. Thankfully, it was short-lived, and I did live to see another day. Before that day was over, a car hit our rental as we sat at a red light. We experienced a few headaches and soreness and were late for our evening speaking engagement. The people were gracious and helped us through the incident; and once again, we lived to see another day.

When morning came, we left at 4:30 a.m. and began our journey home. The drive to the airport had been planned and plotted to make sure we got there in plenty of time to return the rental car and make our flights—until just one decision started a downward domino effect. I thought we had made a wrong turn. Cherylann was not sure and decided to turn around. The car got stuck in gravel and mud. The only way out we could see in the very dark woods was to go down the side of the incline and go back onto the road below. That would have worked, except for the mud we could not see in the dark. I experienced it up to my ankles when the car got stuck. There we were in the dark and the mud. Time was ticking, and we were going to miss our flights. Frustrated with myself because I had a suspicion that we should not have turned around to begin with and it was my fault and because I did not know what to do, I walked away for a second and prayed quietly. I knew that God knew what was going on. I had no clue. He saw us in the depths of the mud, freezing cold, and bad decisions. All I could sense Him saying was to trust Him.

We called our host family and cried out for help. Very graciously, Scott came to our rescue with a truck and a rope and pulled us out. In the meantime, Cherylann had discovered a little road that led to a house, and that house had a paved driveway that led back out to the main road. God had provided a way out. We just could not see it in the dark.

The end of the story is that I barely made my flight. Cherylann missed hers. My flight was delayed to Oklahoma City because, once again, there was fog in the area. Eventually, I made it home, tired and blessed and challenged. We met some genuinely amazing people on our New York adventure. They fed us buffalo wings and provided us with a rental car that we returned caked in mud. They listened to our stories about women and girls in Indonesia and prayed with us and invited us back anytime. And I will be ready to go.

A Trinity of Worship

Growing up as a Southern Baptist preacher's daughter, I had spent my life attending church. Sometimes, we lived in the church parsonage, and it felt like we lived in the church. My earliest memory of going to church was as a five-year-old in Mount Ida, Arkansas. I remember walking up the hill from the parsonage to the church twice a day on Sunday and once on Wednesday to attend all services and activities. And I remember being grumpy because I had to walk up that hill again on a Sunday evening and again miss the broadcast of the movie *The Wizard of Oz*. On Sunday nights, *The Wonderful World of Disney* aired, and I never got to see it. I know, I had a rough childhood. (I did finally see the movie as an adult. I am no longer deprived of Dorothy and her adventures in Oz.)

I think back on all the churches I have been a member of and have attended all of those years. There are way too many to count. I have attended church services in Arkansas, Maryland, Oklahoma, Mexico, Rome, Bangladesh, South Africa, East London, Indonesia, and back to Oklahoma. I loved worshiping with fellow believers in their churches, in their countries, in their heart languages. But first, let me take you to the island of Central Indonesia. It began my recent "Trinity of Worships."

Imagine the inside of a dark, smoke-filled nightclub. This church was started in a club that catered to the nightlife in the evenings; but on Sunday at noon, this place was throbbing with Christian music in both English and Bahasa Indonesian. I attended the service with my She Is Safe co-workers. They welcomed expats, Christians from nearby islands and countries, and the women who worked there each night. If you looked up toward the top of the room, there was a second level decorated with thick, red curtains. Behind them victims of sex trafficking were forced to entertain, in a variety of ways, the patrons of the club. Some girls had been lured from their homes and tricked into a contract to work for a minimum of a year and pay back a loan for which they had not asked.

I have attended there many times. I have spoken on that stage and sat in that audience and sang and prayed and listened to many speakers. I was always grateful to attend and meet the people of that unique church, even though I always wish I had taken my earplugs. I knew I was usually the only grandma in the crowd. I sensed the presence of God in that dark nightclub on an Indonesian island, half a world away.

Come with me now to the second of my "Trinity of Worships." Sit with me in the pew in my stain-glass adorned home church, First Baptist Church, in Duncan, Oklahoma. I sat and sang worship songs and heard a beautiful, challenging sermon by my pastor, Pastor Bryan.

I belong there. I am comfortable there. My family is there. I know the songs. I know when to stand up and sit down. I know the people, and they know me. I feel seen and loved. I miss this place when I am gone, and I am teary-eyed when I return because I was missed and then I was home. I knew the presence of God was there among those precious, servant-hearted people.

Come with me now to the final church in my "Trinity of Worships." Sit with me in a new place I visited—Arch Street First United Methodist Church in Philadelphia, Pennsylvania. No, I was not looking to change denominations, but I loved this church and the morning service in many ways. This church was a short walk from the hotel Johnny and I were staying in while he attended his engineering convention. I thought I would enjoy another cultural experience and attend the service that morning.

The building was built in 1862. Its gray stones and arches and stained-glass windows tell an old, old story. When I walked up to the building, the doorways were blocked by homeless people with "Please Give Anything" signs, their heap of belongings, and some trash scattered around them. When a door opened on the side, I entered and was met with a pungent odor—a musty mixture of sweat and urine. Two homeless people were sleeping on the back pews. About thirty to thirty-five people were scattered throughout the sanctuary, including the vested pastor behind the big, wooden pulpit and the robed choir in the balcony.

Printed on the front of the bulletin, the words defined these people: "A Reconciling Congregation." The banner hung on the side of the wall proudly proclaimed what they were about: "Seek Justice, Love All." This was a people who opened their doors to everyone, fed the hungry, and talked about and did justice in the ways they believed.

I was reminded of the Trinity again because that day was Pentecost Sunday, a day to celebrate the Holy Spirit, the third member of the Holy Trinity. That is what we did—from the opening pipe organ-led hymn to the welcome of "Peace Be with You" and the sermon, in which the pastor asked, "How does the Holy Spirit show up in your life each day?"

The pastor reminded us of three religions and how each celebrated gifts that day—the Jews celebrated the gift of Feasts; Muslims, the gift of Ramadan; and Christians, the gift of the Holy Spirit. I thought about worshiping in a nightclub in Central Indonesia, then my home church, and then this place—all so different. Did I agree with all of what they did? No. Did some of what they did and say push against my sense of what was right and wrong? It did. But did I feel the presence of God in each place? Absolutely.

At the close of the service, the end of my "Trinity of Worships," the choir led in the old spiritual hymn, "Every Time I Feel the Spirit." The congregation clapped and joined in on the chorus. The pastor closed with a challenge for us to go into the world and bring peace.

When I walked out the door, the homeless people were still there, just as the trafficked girls were still at the nightclub in Central Indonesia, and just as the comfortable are in the pews in my hometown. And I am encouraged to take my "Trinity of Worships" into the streets and all over the world.

Do You Know That Feeling?

You are sitting alone quietly, and you feel like someone is staring at you. That happened to me recently. I looked up, and our eyes met for a brief second. Then she looked down again. What was she doing, sitting there alone staring at me?

I had eaten lunch earlier that day about three miles away on the north side of Oklahoma City. I had spent a leisurely lunchtime alone in one of my favorite food chains enjoying a sandwich and soup. Then I read for a while and watched people around me—some in their nice suits talking business with each other, some eating their chicken salads while enjoying conversation with friends. I finished lunch and my errands around town but still had time to spare before my appointment at the health clinic to get my typhoid vaccination for my upcoming international trip. I drove toward my destination and stopped at a fast-food place for a cup of coffee and filled the time reading and sipping my java. That was when her eyes met mine.

It struck me how different types of people live within the same city only a few miles apart but can be worlds apart. There were no suits and ties in this establishment. It was mostly working men finishing their shifts with sweat-stained and grease-smeared shirts. A few elderly people were sitting alone slowly finishing their small orders of French fries. I heard at least three different languages—Spanish, Hindi, and something else I could not distinguish. I wondered where she was from.

A few moments after I sat down with my coffee, I saw her enter from a side door and slide into a booth about five booths away from me. She was an older black woman wearing a heavy jacket, perspiring freely on this warm September afternoon. I made some assumptions about her—a homeless woman with nowhere to go in the middle of the afternoon. Knowing the fast-food joint would offer her a cool respite from the warm temperatures and a place to sit down for a few minutes, she slipped in through the side door and hunched down in the booth in the back of the place out of full view of watchful eyes at the front counter. She did not order any food or drink. I wondered when the last time was that she had anything to eat or drink.

I looked back at my book on my electronic device and reabsorbed myself in my reading for a few minutes more, glanced at my watch, and relaxed a while before my appointment. I looked at the woman again. This time, as she sat slumped over the table, her eyes were closed. I wondered where she would sleep tonight. After a few more minutes, as I finished my coffee, I looked again toward the woman; and she was gone. I did not see her leave or where she went. I had not done anything to help her or get to know her. It made me wonder why lives intersect that way and what it was that I should have done or should have learned from that brief shared moment in time with an unseen woman.

It made me wonder why some people are blessed in life to wear nice clothes and eat overpriced sandwiches and why others, only a few miles away, sit silently alone in a sticky fast-food booth and stare into space and sometimes into the eyes of strangers. Next time, I wondered if I would be brave enough to burst the bubble of my safety zone, enter her world, walk across the restaurant, and just say, "Hi, what's your favorite meal here? I'd like to buy you something to eat." Then I would sit and watch her eat her burger and listen to her story. I had a feeling I would get another opportunity at some point in time; the next time I sensed someone staring at me, I hoped I would be brave enough to just walk across the room.

That was a few years ago. What have I learned from this post-dated encounter? Recently, I finished my morning shopping trip in a nearby city with lunch at a favorite soup and sandwich restaurant. It was nothing fancy, but it always had delicious food. I ordered my club sandwich and broccoli cheddar soup and sat down and awaited my order to be brought to my table. I sipped my diet cola, pulled out my smartphone, and logged in. As I sat waiting, I noticed the lady in the booth next to me did not seem to be getting her food. She was alone and wearing a lot of clothes for an unseasonably warm late-winter day. She only drank a bottle of juice she had apparently brought into the restaurant with her. *Curious*, I thought.

My food order came, and I resumed reading social media posts on my phone and enjoyed my lunch. Occasionally, I glanced to my left. The lady was still there. She still had no food; she was just sitting and sipping her juice. *Still curious.*

I finished my lunch quickly and headed out the door to my car. I had things to do when I got home, so I needed to be on my way. And then I saw it—her cart. The lady in the booth next to me sat by a window, and her cart was sitting where she could keep an eye on it. Everything she owned and valued was stuffed into that cart. She had come into the restaurant to take a break from her wanderings. I did not know anything about her and what her life was like, but I knew it contrasted greatly with my lifestyle. I had shopped that morning and put stuff into my new car to drive home. Her shopping was gleaned from who-knows-where and stuffed into an overflowing "borrowed" cart.

I did not do anything to help her. I could have gone back into the restaurant and offered to pay for her meal or something—anything. But I did not. I got in my new car and drove home. And I could not get her out of my head. I am not sure when I will learn my lesson on how to respond to people in obvious need, look into the eyes of strangers, and make a new friend.

"What's Happening?"

My thoughts for our Toronto mission team of four from First Baptist Church were these two words as the defining phrase from our five-day discovery trip. Pastors Bryan, Jordan, Matthew, and I spent a lot of time in our rental van en route to many venues to meet with church planters and missionaries to understand their calling in this massive city. We desired to find out how our church could partner with them and to assist them as they fulfilled that calling. We were asking the question all week: "What's happening here, and how can we help?"

As we traveled, my seat of honor in the van was the front passenger location. Pastor Bryan drove, and Jordan and Matt sat behind us. One evening, as we drove back to our hotel after a visit to the home of our host missionaries, Bryan put on his signal to turn left through a busy intersection. As he started the turn, I glanced up in just enough time to see a car careening toward us—or, more accurately, toward me on the passenger side. I did not have enough time to see my life flashing before me. All I could utter in my quiet voice was, "What's happening?"

At that moment, Bryan looked up from a distraction from the car navigation panel and realized he did not have a protected left turn signal, immediately corrected the situation, and we all emerged safely. *Whew.* That was way too close.

In the moment on the other side of the intersection, when he realized what had just transpired, Bryan burst out laughing. It seemed his history of sticky driving situations and how his wife would have responded in the same situation compared to mine were remarkably different.

"I'm going to tell Shonda there is another way to respond to my driving!"

By then, we were all laughing.

I replied, "I don't think I would have been so calm if it had been Johnny driving."

And from that moment in time, "What's happening?" had a unique situational meaning for the four of us.

I found myself asking that question as we met with pastors from Sri Lanka, Nepal, the Philippines, and the Congo (and his wife from Russia). What's happening that you would come from your countries so far away and plant yourself in Canada among your people there and among people from so many nations? Even to the pastor from Mississippi, we asked, "What's happening in your life that you would answer the call to uproot your family and plant yourself in a foreign place in the middle of a pandemic?"

These are questions we all need to ponder. What's happening in your life that enables you to see people in need? In what ways can you make a difference?

7
Learning from Unseen People in Planes, Trains, and Automobiles

MY MULTIPLE MISSION TRIPS HAVE served as a testing and training ground throughout my life to see the unseen. I recommend everyone take advantage of a church mission trip with the goal of serving those in need and sharing the love of Christ.

I have been to some amazing locations, both in North America and internationally. However, you must know in advance that I did not go on these trips primarily as a tourist, except for one in the list below. I did go with groups of people, but they were not tourist groups in which I was their guide. I was their team leader; and I did, most of the time, allow them one day to wear sunglasses, strap on their cameras and fanny packs, and look totally like geeky American tourists. But for the most part, our days were not spent sipping overpriced drinks in trendy coffee shops, or shopping for trinkets in souvenir shops, or lounging by the swimming pool or on the beach; no, my trips to beautiful, historic, tropical destinations were replete with making sure each person had their passport and knew when to meet back at the bus and what their ministry assignment for the day was.

The following are my top ten favorite places I have been. I cannot list all the locations I took mission teams to, but almost all of them were good. They were definitely all unique, and I pray that God was honored in all of them. Following this list are ten practical ways to see and serve the unseen.

Grand Canyon, Arizona

This was the final destination after a week spent in Phoenix with a mission team. I have to say, it was one of the easiest trips ever as far as actual mission work goes. However, at the beginning of the trip, I literally thought I was going to die due to a snowstorm that hit at the end of a very, very long drive in a crowded church van. After slipping and sliding for hours on a very scary interstate, we did not die, by God's grace, and lived to pass out flyers, prayer walk, and wash car windshields in Phoenix. And then, as a gift from God, at the end of the week, we were allowed to stand at the edge of the Grand Canyon for about an hour. It was big, spectacular, and overwhelming. When we were all back in the van headed east toward Oklahoma, we were thankful for seeing one of the wonders of the world that God had made and shared with us.

New York City, New York

I saw the city of Lady Liberty, Times Square, and Central Park with about twenty teenagers. Thankfully, sightseeing in Manhattan only took one day of our week in New York. Most of the time was spent on subways underneath Queens and Brooklyn on our way to sites where we taught English as a Second Language to women from India and Bangladesh. We ate pizza at Mario's and painted faces and made balloon animals for children in a Brooklyn city park. At Mario's Pizzeria, near the location where we stayed, I remember Mario being fascinated that we were from Oklahoma. I am sure he imagined cowboys and Indians, saloons and gunfights on the street. He asked, "Do you ride your horses to work?" I smiled and thought, *Well, maybe I would if I owned one.* I imagined a horse tied up to a tree at the church building where I worked.

Banff, Alberta, Canada

This is the one and only location on this list that was not a mission trip. It was where Johnny and I spent our twenty-fifth anniversary. I loved the experience of standing on a glacier and experiencing snow on July 30. I knew we were not in Oklahoma anymore! It was so beautiful—a breathtaking vista at every turn in the Rocky Mountain road. I would go back in a heartbeat.

San Francisco, California

This was not a mission trip destination either but the beginning of a She Is Safe trip to Indonesia. In just a few hours, before we had to go to the airport to meet our international flight, my She Is Safe co-worker, Katy, and her husband, Greg, drove me through the highlights of San Francisco. I loved eating pastries at their favorite city bakery, driving down the famous curvy Lombard Street, and, of course, savoring a priceless view of the Golden Gate Bridge.

Washington, D.C.

This was both a mission trip destination and a family vacation location. You remember that I spent twelve weeks in the Maryland/D.C. area when I was a college student. There is something majestic about standing on the Mall and seeing the Capitol, the Smithsonian museums, the Washington Monument, and Lincoln Memorial—all in one 360-degree turn. It was also fascinating as you look at totally American shrines to hear the babble of languages from Africa and India and Mexico, all looking at and admiring the same monuments.

South Africa

One of my favorite memories from all my trips was standing at the "End of the Earth." It certainly felt like it as we stood on the rocky edge of the Cape of Good Hope. South Africa is a diverse and beautiful country with beautiful people but with a questionable and violent past. I am so happy that my memories of this country were spent with a mixture of people called the Coloured People of the Northern Cape. These were people who did not have a people, people no one wanted—but people God saw, loved, and called His own. I would go back in a heartbeat.

Bangladesh, South Asia

One of the places that overwhelmed my senses in every way was Dhaka, Bangladesh. It was loud, hot, vibrant, and colorful. There were people everywhere. It was pulsating with people. Drive a few hours northeast to the district of Sylhet and you find beautiful, lush tea gardens—steamy hot and a deep green garden of delight. Some of the most hospitable, beautiful people are in this country and enjoyed serving us their famous tea.

London, England

This location wins as the place where I have taken the most mission teams. Seven times, I have taken groups to see Big Ben, the Tower of London, and Buckingham Palace. My favorite touristy spot of all time is Westminster Abbey. I just love standing and looking up at the amazing architecture and listening to the hum of the big red buses going by. I love the mix of languages of the people—both Brits and all the tongues of the tourists mixed together. I love the stroll through history planted within the walls and floors of the abbey. One time, I happened upon a boys' choir singing the "Hallelujah" chorus. I will not forget that. Yet most of our time those weeks were spent in the east part of that historic city among South Asian people who had made this rainy, cold city their home. I loved visiting them in their homes and meeting them on the streets, listening to their stories of pain and hope.

Rome, Italy

Of all the locations where I have taken mission teams, this is the one location I want to go back to and not take nine other adults to do Vacation Bible School and refugee outreach. I want to take one adult—my husband—so we can stroll through the history that you find down every narrow street. I want to watch him enjoy the history of the Coliseum and the Forum, without making sure we do not lose seven other people on our frantic journey to the Metro. One day, we will go back and toss our coins into Trevi Fountain. It was supposed to happen on our thirtieth anniversary, but we were celebrating the birth of our first grandchild instead. We celebrated at home and held baby Leah in our arms. A tour through St. Paul's Cathedral does not beat that.

Indonesia

What a diverse country and people. From the lush, thick jungles of Sumatra to the beaches of islands in Central Indonesia, this is a country that has truly captured my heart—not because I love water but because God had allowed me to work with amazing people who cared deeply about precious women and girls in this country, women who lived lives of oppression or poverty, abuse or exploitation. The beauty of the country is tempered with the darkness of the shadows of evil and anger and sadness. The travel to get there is long. It is literally halfway around the world from my Oklahoma home. Travel in the country can be strenuous, but the rewards of seeing the smiles of children and the joy of women as they work together was truly priceless.

The challenge for us as we travel, whether on a mission trip, for business, or for pleasure, is the following:

1. Take time to see people normally overlooked including servers, cashiers, maintenance workers, taxi drivers, or cleaning crews.
2. Realize that they are not there just to serve and make us comfortable, but they are real people with real needs.
3. Humbly ask yourself: How can I help them feel seen, valuable, and needed? How can I treat them the way I would want to be treated if I were them? How do they deserve to be treated? "And as you wish that others would do to you, do so to them" (Luke 6:31).
4. Offer a smile.

5. Learn their names.
6. Say, "Thank you."
7. Engage in conversation as appropriate. Ask about their family, their work, etc.
8. Offer an encouragement. Unseen people are accustomed to being verbally degraded or ridiculed. Do not be that person that makes them feel that way.
9. Remember that God sees everyone the same. He has just placed us in different locations and positions.
10. Remember if unseen people are not seen by followers of Jesus, who will see them as the treasures they truly are?

I traveled with my husband on a business trip to Philadelphia a few years ago. When Johnny attended his conference, I often stayed in the hotel room to do some work. On those mornings, the staff cleaning attendant came to do her job to clean our room. In those few brief encounters, I learned her name was Mary. She had been working at her job in this downtown Philadelphia hotel for several years. It took her an hour to get to work and then back home each day. I could tell she was proud of the work she did. I pray for Mary often and wonder if she still works there and if she found a relationship with God.

Get Your Passport and Use It

When I served as minister of missions at my church, I made a plea every year for members to get their passports and be prepared to use them to travel to the nations to share the love of Christ. I got my first passport in 2000 and received my first international stamp from a country not at the top of major tourist attractions. I got prepared to go to Bolivia, South America, to serve with a team from our church to work with missionary children. We conducted a Vacation Bible School for them, while their parents attended their annual training event.

I remember flying to the country over the lush Andes mountains. That week, I watched parrots fly over my head. I was standing in their natural habitat. I watched a sloth do nothing in a tree in one of the city parks. I experienced the dedication that families had to say yes to God and go where He sent them. In this case, it was into the jungles and the cities in the depths of South America.

I have been through three passports now and use a Global Entry card that gets me in and out of the United States more quickly. I have learned much since my first international trip to Bolivia, and I still encourage everyone to get their passport and use it.

A Book and a Burden

I could not get the stories out of my head. I was serving in my church as missions minister, but I knew in my heart it was time to move on. I loved organizing local projects to help meet the needs of people in our community—including a free food and clothing ministry, a block party for the immediate area around our church, a ministry of giving away bottles of cold water, and a face-painting at a city summer event. I loved leading teams of church members to go around the world from Mexico to Rome, from South Africa to Bangladesh. That season of my life was coming to an end, and I knew it.

Each day, as I sat in my office and looked over my planning calendar, I dealt with an unsettledness that I could not explain. Yet I did not know what was next. And then, I read a book. I could not get the stories out of my head, and they found their way into my heart.

I saw the books advertised on a site I frequented to gather up-to-date mission information. The books were *Forgotten Girls* and *Daughters of Hope*. My background of writing missions curriculum for the Woman's Missionary Union and years of cross-cultural traveling had primed me to order these books. I read them and sat stunned, trying to absorb what was on the pages.

The introduction to *Forgotten Girls* told the story of a baby girl born in an Asian country. Because she was a girl and unwanted and unvalued, the father buried her alive in their backyard. The baby's tender-hearted grandfather quickly found an opportunity to rescue her and get her to safety; and eventually, a family adopted her.

The first chapter in the book left me with a burden. It told the story of a four-year-old Indonesian girl abandoned by her family and given to the village witch. This little girl was forced to do work beyond her capability to perform, and she was severely abused—beaten, cut, dirty, and starved. The story told of corrupt police who did not care to help an insignificant little girl. As I turned the pages, the burden in my heart grew. Who would help her? A local ministry leader rescued the girl and gave her hope and a home and a chance to be a little girl again.[13]

I read the other stories quickly as they told encounters of forgotten, unseen girls around the world. I knew I had to do something. I contacted the organization that had advertised the books: She Is Safe. Through much prayer and phone and personal interviews with the directors of She Is Safe, I knew what was next for me. A year after I read those books, I found myself standing in the same village where that story of the little girl and witch took place. I met the woman who rescued the girl, stayed in her home, and developed a deep and lasting partnership. I returned to the country fourteen times during the years I served as country director for Indonesia. Only God could do that. He gave me a holy discontent, and He replaced it with a book and a burden. My life has not been the same since. And I am grateful.

Thoughts the Night before a Journey to the Other Side of the Word

It is almost time to go again. My next trip to Indonesia with She Is Safe awaits. Sometimes, I wonder why I would want to put myself through the "joys" that are international travel, including crowded planes; curvy, nausea-inducing

---

13 Kay Marshall Strom and Michele Rickett, *Forgotten Girls: Stories of Hope and Courage* (Lisle: IVP Press, 2014).

mountain roads; and heat and humidity thick enough to slice. I love my work, but my work is challenging on many levels. It is amazing that an introvert who has claustrophobic issues would want to be enclosed in an airplane for twenty-four hours one way and go to a crowded Asian country. It must have been a God-thing. And even though I believed I was called by God to do that work at that time in my life, it did not mean it was easy, safe, or comfortable.

There were many things I found challenging about the international travel part of my job. For one, I did not enjoy traveling by plane. Too many people were way too close to me. I like people—I honestly do—but not when their seat reclines into my face and when they snore loudly and get stupid and sloppy when they drink too much. I also hate packing. It is just too much work to cram two weeks' worth of my life into bags. It is not like there is a convenience store down the street where I am going. It was stressful to remember to pack everything like medicines and toothbrushes and chocolate.

I also miss my family and my "creature comforts" when I am away. I mean, why would you not miss sweet, smiling faces like my grandchildren's? Plus, I wanted my comfy recliner, bed, and bathroom. After twenty-four hours of traveling, all I wanted to do was take a shower and put up my feet. It was those times when I knew there was no place like home.

As mentioned, I love people. But since I am an introvert, people zap my energy. And there is no getting away from everyone on most trips. I am worn out at the end of these marathon journeys. It is not my favorite part of traveling.

So why go? Well, I go for the people. Wait, I just said they made me tired. They did, but I absolutely loved the Indonesian people I worked with. They were like family. In fact, my Indonesian family "adopted" me and gave me their last name. I loved that I felt so at home there. I treasured those people. They were my favorite. Also, the She Is Safe staff was my family; and usually one or more traveled with me or met me there. We worked together, laughed together, and enjoyed being together. I loved working with people who felt like family.

I also go because of the beauty of Indonesia. It is a fascinating combination of beautiful landscapes, including volcanoes (some of which remain active) and jungles that include monkeys, elephants, pythons, and orangutans. I once saw a gigantic python curled up on the bank of the lazy river feeding into the Indian Ocean. A beautiful orangutan mama hanging out in her Sumatran habitat with her baby made me think they could have been in the slick, colorful pages of *National Geographic*.

Indonesia is a fascinating blend of beautiful people, flavorful spices, interesting food, and many islands. Indonesia consists of seventeen thousand islands. It is fascinating to think that a people created a culture out of that many islands. I also love new experiences. I learn new things; meet new people; and see, feel, taste, smell, and touch lives in a whole new way than in Duncan, Oklahoma. And I love my work with She Is Safe. Helping women and girls be safe and free from abuse and slavery is worth the inconveniences Now, I have to go finish packing and get some sleep. I am ready to do this one more time.

From Where I Sit

"So, what do you do that requires you to travel so much internationally?"

It was a simple question I had been asked many times by curious strangers. On this particular occasion, the question came from our cell phone salesman while he was uploading media files onto my new smartphone. I explained my job with She Is Safe as country director for Indonesia. I explained the purpose of our organization and how we help international co-workers prevent, rescue, and restore women and girls from abuse and exploitation.

"Cool," he responded. He continued to punch the keys on my shiny new phone. "I hear about people doing stuff like that, but I've never met one before."

There is so much more I want to explain to people about this fascinating work; but I usually try to keep it short, since most people get through listening before I get through talking.

I had just returned from my latest trip a few days before this conversation at the cell phone store. I had talked with women who were overcoming poverty and physical abuse to earn a living through self-help groups and micro-loans. I sat across the table from a fifteen-year-old girl, who had only recently been rescued from sex trafficking. It was amazing work that I had a little part in doing.

The funny thing was, in between these fascinating personal encounters, I sat. I sat a lot. My coworker and fellow traveler on many of my trips, Katy, and I made a long list about the locations that required us to sit as we traveled globally. I am sure there were brilliant ideas that emerged from those hours of sitting; at least, I hope they did. Here is a list that Katy and I devised while sitting in an airport terminal in Central Indonesia, waiting to board the first flight of our trip back home:

Places we have sat as we traveled:

1. In airport terminals
2. In airplanes on domestic flights (aisle seat, please)
3. In airplanes on international flights (I really have to have an aisle seat for flights totaling twenty-four hours.)
4. In restaurants, consuming all kinds of delicious food, often involving fish and rice
5. In cars, often hoping that the anti-nausea medication will do what it claims to do
6. In our host homes, enjoying great conversations, making life-long friends, and often smiling a lot waiting for the interpretation to make its way back to us.
7. On floors, visiting women's groups in rural settings.
8. On the beds in our rooms, in homes or hotels, with a variety of mattresses.
9. In various rooms around tables discussing ministry plans (sometimes for up to ten hours in one day)

10. On a boat in Indonesia on a stormy sea
11. On airport shuttle vehicles
12. In coffee shops—one of my favorite places to sit
13. In the lobbies of hotels, waiting for our host to come for us
14. On the porches of our host homes, sometimes relaxing, sometimes taking photos, sometimes photos being taken of us, sometimes getting eaten by a myriad of insects
15. In church services
16. In a car in a traffic jam for five hours on a mountain in Indonesia

You get the idea. We sit a lot. I would like to think that the adage is true; that *great things come to those who wait* also applies to great things come to those who *sit*. I know for certain that the people I have met, the stories I have heard, and the challenges I have encountered have been worth all the hours of sitting and waiting. But if it is okay, I think I will wait awhile before I board another plane and sit and travel to the other side of the world. I will sit here, in my comfy recliner, and rest.

Oh, the great places you'll go if you step into God's mission work, and you will have great stories to tell. You will see the unseen; but first, you have to sit!

The Kindness of Strangers in an Airport

It was not a place you normally found an outpouring of kindness. Everyone was either in a hurry, tired of waiting for delayed flights, or glued to some type of electronic device. I found myself waiting in line to talk to a representative from the airline at their customer service desk in the San Francisco airport. I had completed my very long flights from India to Singapore, to Seoul, South Korea, and now to San Francisco. I only needed to connect with short flights to Denver, then on to Oklahoma City. But no, that little flight to Denver had a delay that would make me miss my connection. All I wanted to do was go to sleep. Instead, I found myself in a line of tired, angry, determined passengers waiting to resolve their travel issues and get to their destinations.

Finally, it was my turn. I did not have to wait as long as some people because I flew frequently and had a plastic card from the airline that proved it. I took my few perks when I could get them. I presented my passport and my dilemma to the next available agent. She looked like she had been at the job for a long while and saw no end in sight as the line of disgruntled, displaced passengers continued to grow. She smiled at me, regardless, and started punching keys on her computer keyboard to see what she could do to fix my problem. Nothing was happening anytime soon.

"Doesn't look like an easy fix," I mumbled to her.

She smiled again and continued to click her keyboard keys. "Well, I could . . . " She rattled off a few options, none of which would get me home that night. She decided on an option for a direct flight the next morning; but because my flight had not been canceled, only delayed, she could not offer me a free hotel room for the night, only a coupon for a discount. I just wanted to sleep.

She looked at my recent travel itinerary and asked, "What were you doing in India, anyway?"

I smiled and said, "And in Indonesia before that." I briefly told her about my work with She Is Safe and how we worked in areas of the world where women and girls were abused and exploited. She told me what she knew about human trafficking and about a recent documentary she had seen. All of this conversation was happening while anxious passengers behind me were waiting.

Then she said, "It's good work you do. We're going to take care of you." She got busy making a few more phone calls; and several minutes later, I was handed information for my free hotel room and food voucher for the evening, along with instructions on where to meet the hotel shuttle. I marveled at the kindness of a stranger bonding with me over a counter in an airport. Thank You, God. All I wanted to do was sleep.

The next morning, after a few hours of sleep, some phone calls to my family, and a free continental breakfast, I found myself back at the same airport, in the same terminal, waiting for my flight. I discovered that my seat on the direct flight home was upgraded to first class. This was not something that normally happened to me, so I was feeling good about my final flight to be with my family.

In the meantime, I settled in to wait for my gate to open. I sat next to a young man with a long beard. We began exchanging small talk. I soon discovered he had been in the airport all night because he accidentally missed his flight. He described the numerous ways of entertaining himself in a deserted airport during the long night and how impossible it was to sleep on the plastic seats when security announcements continued to loop throughout the wee hours. He was a commercial fisherman on his way back from Hawaii and headed home to Oregon to his fishing business, his wife, and four daughters.

I told him briefly about She Is Safe, and he immediately connected with me because of his love for his daughters and desire to keep them safe. He had kind eyes and smiled through his tangled whiskers as he talked about them. As my flight finally opened for boarding, he thumped his chest and said, "I've got you right here in my heart. Thank you for the work you do." Thank You, God, for the kindness of strangers in an airport.

On the flight, I found myself seated in my comfortable first-class seat next to a rather large man returning from a business trip to China. I am sure we could have exchanged stories about our Asian adventures in travel. Instead, all we wanted to do was sleep.

The Question

It would happen again in a few days. I would take my passport and carefully packed bags, board a plane and start my journey halfway around the world—twenty-four hours on a plane. As usual, about this point in my countdown to take-off, I asked myself the question, *Why am I doing this again?*

Why am I leaving my wonderful husband and family, my cozy home, and comfortable American life? Why am I trading it for two weeks of tight spaces on planes and cars and everyplace else? I would be immersed into a culture that was fascinating but foreign, going to a location that was lush and tropical, yet mysterious, where I would communicate in mixtures of unknown words, gestures, and mostly, "How do you say . . . " or, "I'm sorry, I don't understand."

Maybe I just will not go this time. Do you think anyone would notice if I did not show up? And before I self-destructed into a puddle of doubt, worry, and stomach pain, I remembered why I went. Her name was Beti.[14]

As I prepared to travel, I recalled the story of a four-year-old girl, abandoned by her parents. The only person in the village who would take a little "worthless" female was the local witch doctor. She was unspeakably cruel to Beti—beating her when she did not do the chores correctly, cutting gashes into her head that was covered by her hair. As I read, I could hear her cry as she was chained outside. Even the police did not care to help the little girl. She was overlooked, unseen, and voiceless—until a hero appeared in the form of a little, yet fiercely passionate, woman leader of a nearby ministry. She stepped in, rescued Beti, and found a loving, nurturing home for her.

But the story for me did not end there. About a year after I initially read that story, I stood in the exact location where that story originated in Sumatra, Indonesia. It was then that I learned that little Beti was now eight years old and had grown up happy and healthy and loved to dance. She was well-loved by all. That is how Beti's story continues today.

That is why I packed my bags, said my goodbyes, and went again. It was because of little girls like Beti. It was because of many women and little girls who lived desperate lives of abuse, poverty, exploitation, and neglect. They are my reason for going—to help their lives have happy endings, to partner with ministry leaders who were making a difference every day preventing harm to them or rescuing and restoring them to live lives of hope filled with

---

14   Strom, ibid.

possibilities of peaceful futures. It was worth the price for me to board that plane, test my patience and pocketbook, and be there. I could provide help, encouragement, and prayers and point them to the only One Who gives lasting hope.

Going Wide

As I prepare to travel again internationally in the coming weeks, I remember some of my past journeys. One of my favorite things about traveling was worshiping with followers of Jesus. It was amazing to me that wherever believers go, they find instant connections with one another. That was especially true as we worshipped together. Even when I could not understand what was being said, the heart from which it was communicated was completely understood. There was a common bond when we worshipped the same God Who is invisible and unexplainable.

In a border town in Mexico was a simple, impromptu worship time before our mission team left to travel home. Our student minister strummed his guitar and led in English choruses. Our Spanish-speaking friends sang along in Spanish, offering sweet sounds of praise together. In South Africa, a small, wooden-framed shanty sat in the backyard of church members. A single lightbulb dangled from the ceiling. It was cold, and I could not understand Afrikaans; but the fellowship was sweet, and the bond was strong.

In a community near Birmingham, England, a group of South Asian believers met in a location that was furnished with pillows on the floor. Incense burned, and prayers were offered in languages I have not heard. They were both a sweet aroma. In the living room of friends in East London, England, worship was led in English by a new friend from India. Sitting in the circle were believers and seekers from other South Asian countries. Children from the United States and Britain and South Asia, all enjoying being children together, joined in the singing. It was beautiful music. In a weather-worn, classic cathedral in central Rome, where believers from all over the world gathered, a visiting choir provided music with handbells. The rich tones bounced off the vaulted ceilings. It was beautiful music.

Each time, we were treated to delicious food following the services—homemade tortillas, carnitas, curries of all kinds. I even brought home the church cookbook from Rome Baptist Church containing yummy Italian recipes. There were many other locations and people I will not name here; but all of them were sweet and beautiful, and I will forever remember those places and unseen people.

8
Looking the Unseen in the Eyes

MY TRAVELS HAVE LED ME to many places mostly unseen by travelers, such as Bolivia, South America, the poorest country on this continent. About eighty percent of the rural population lives below the poverty line. I would not exactly describe it as a tourist destination. It was my first international trip that required a passport. It was there that I experienced what it meant to have *agua sin gas* (water without gas), to survive crazy drivers in traffic circles, to listen to the never-ending honking of horns, and to experience the graciousness and hospitality of South American people. I went there to help with a Vacation Bible School for missionary children. It was an experience and a place that dug deep into my heart. It was not a place many people choose to go to willingly. So why did I want to go there?

Dhaka, Bangladesh, was my first visit to an Asian country. Bangladesh is the fourth poorest South Asian nation. Once again, I went there to serve with international workers. I remember sitting in a car alone while everyone else on my team went into a shop. The throbbing throng of people seemed to press against the vehicle, and I felt like I could not breathe. There were so many people. But as I got acquainted with Bangladeshi people, I experienced a warmth and friendliness like I had never known. I watched as my hosts ate the eyeballs of the fish we were served. I felt the stares of people who had most likely never seen a person with skin as white as mine. They were precious people, and I quickly fell in love with them. I visited the country twice. The tea gardens in the northern part of the country were luscious; the rice, never-ending; the immersion into the Muslim way of life, fascinating. Still, it was not a place many people choose to go to willingly. So why did I want to go there?

I fell in love with Sumatra, Indonesia. Indonesia is another Muslim-majority nation. I went there to serve with partners of She Is Safe. The memory of being on a boat in the dark is a memory seared deep into my being—along with visiting women and children in remote villages multiple times in their humble homes; sitting with them on the floor, drinking their strong, earthy Sumatran coffee; and eating mounds of white rice. This is a country people go to willingly as tourists, but that was not the case with many of the places I went. So why did I want to go there?

Here is the short answer: because God is there. He has always been there. He called me to go to the jungles and the cities of Bolivia, to the streets of Dhaka, to the Indonesian island you will never hear of, and to so many other places to meet fascinating unseen people. I would not trade a bit of it. It reminds me of these words:

> Where shall I go from your Spirit? Or where shall I flee from your presence? If I ascend to heaven, you are there! If I make my bed in Sheol, you are there! If I take the wings of the morning and dwell in the uttermost parts of the sea, even there your hand shall lead me, and your right hand shall hold me. If I say, "Surely the darkness shall cover me, and the light about me be night," even the darkness is not dark to you; the night is bright as the day, for darkness is as light with you (Psalm 139:7-12).

He is already there. He is always there, waiting for me. He is waiting for you, too. Where do you want to go? What unseen people do you want to meet?

On a Boat in the Dark in Indonesia

Was this really happening? I was facing a surreal, suspenseful sensory overload. I sat in the front of the motorboat, speeding across the ocean in the waters surrounding Sumatra, the sea-salted wind streaming through my hair. Was it real? Was I half a world away in a small boat with eight other people headed for the shores of the big Indonesian island?

The tropical beauty was too much to absorb—small green islands topped with palm trees dotted the seascape, and puffy white clouds and a setting orange sun painted the western sky behind us. I stated the obvious to Katy, my fellow teammate seated beside me, "I'm on a boat . . . in Indonesia."

It was so hard to process the reality and believe we were there. When a brilliant rainbow formed in front of us, God seemed to proclaim, "This place that I've created is truly a treasure, full of people who need to know Me." However, the mystical beauty soon faded as the sun set and we found ourselves on the sea in the dark, with only a small flashlight the boat captain used to scan the dangers directly in front of us.

I had asked many people to pray for me on that day. I do not like water that much, as you already know. I am okay being on the water in a boat or wading along the safe shore, but I have no desire to be immersed in it. It is a phobia I need to conquer, but I did not want to deal with it at that moment in time. As always, God was faithful; and we made it back to the dock. I did not experience an unexpected swim in the dark waters.

That was only one remarkable moment on that trip to Indonesia. The team of three She Is Safe sisters and I traveled with shared many amazing moments along our journey. We watched women in self-help groups sewing, crocheting, and making soap to sell to earn much-needed income for their families. They saved money to start businesses, to pay school fees for their children, and to earn respect from their husbands and village leaders. We tasted and tried to swallow a small bite of durian fruit. I do not ever recall gagging on food, but I just could not get past the pungent odor. I will never try that again.

Another adventure was when we tossed about in a storm in a fifteen-passenger airplane. Our ministry partner grabbed my hand and started to sing a hymn. I experienced the great faithfulness of our Father as He guided the pilots to a safe landing.

We also heard the gut-wrenching stories of a mother and her seventeen-year-old pregnant daughter-in-law who were both continually beaten and abused by their husbands. We encouraged the young woman to find safety to protect her unborn child. We listened through tears and prayed that God would provide comfort and peace and change the actions of men who caused such harm and sadness. I have introduced you to Rina in other stories in these pages.

Together, we traveled back up the mountain in Sumatra, up the winding and bumpy roads that caused us to continually sway into each other and be very grateful for a dosage of anti-nausea medication. On one of those journeys on a Sunday morning, we worshiped together, singing hymns in harmony—Indonesian sisters and a brother and American sisters joining together to offer praise to our common King. I loved impromptu worship services, where language and culture are not a barrier because we serve the same Savior.

We sat in a crowded car after receiving the message that my daddy had passed away. We all worked together to put a plan in motion that would allow me to arrive home a day earlier than scheduled just in time to attend his funeral. I knew so many people were praying—from Oklahoma to London to Indonesia and many locations in between—for connections to be made and travels to be smooth. God certainly heard and answered those prayers, and my amazing journey ended beside the casket of my sweet daddy. My mother, sister, and brother gave me the gift of support to go ahead with my She Is Safe trip, even if he should die before I returned. I will forever be grateful for that gift of freedom to go and serve in the way God has provided for me. I certainly hoped Daddy would have been healed, and I would get to see him again completely well. But that was not meant to be. I am forever grateful that God gave me His grace to both go and serve and also return to be with my family on the day we said goodbye to Daddy.

I am thankful to everyone who made the adventure to Indonesia happen for me—those who provided support through financial gifts and words of encouragement and persistent prayers. I wondered about the next trip. Would I again find myself on a boat in the dark n Indonesia, experiencing another journey into the land of brilliant rainbows, tropical storms, and winding mountain roads? Who knows what great places you will go to when God provides open doors? Who knows how many unseen people you will discover?

What Do I Say?

It was a legitimate question: "What are you going to say?" I did not have a legitimate answer. Our mission team of four were in a village in South Africa on the Northern Cape. We stood before a small congregation of people who had endured great pain through the years—outcasts because they were neither white nor black. They were a people of mixed ancestry, and no one wanted to claim them. As a white Christian from North America, I had not known the pain of being ostracized for my skin color.

The mission team members I stood with had collectively experienced the burden of alcoholic parents, the pain of divorce, and the unanswered questions of an adopted child. Then there was me. I was the third child in a family where my parents loved each other. I had a loving husband, two great children, and a ministry job I loved. I had known nothing of the pain and suffering that life offered.

That trip was many years ago, and the question my team member asked me still haunts me. What did I say? I do not remember. I think I offered some kind of encouragement to the congregation, introduced our team, and let them speak from their years of experience and wisdom.

What did I say as I traveled with She Is Safe when I sat on the floor of a humble home in a village in Sumatra and listened as women told their stories of when their husbands beat them out of an alcoholic rage? What did I say to little girls who were responsible for caring for their younger brothers and sisters because their mothers had to work long hours doing back-breaking farm labor? What did I say to our Indonesian ministry leader who had repeatedly walked into danger because she was heartbroken for her neighbors? Who am I to provide words of wisdom and comfort when I have not known the pain and the joy of suffering as they had?

Recently, I have experienced the pain of leaving a comfortable job and stepping into the unknown and putting myself into uncertain international situations. I have lost my parents, who died and left me with a deep sadness that I have never known before. I have watched my husband being carefully placed on a helicopter that medi-flighted him to a hospital to undergo back surgery. I have walked with my therapy dog into the halls of nursing homes and watched people die a little more every day. I would like to think my journeys, recent losses, changes, and griefs have helped equip me to hear and see people in ways I have never known before. I am thankful that my life so far has not dealt me devastating losses and unknowable grief. I am grateful for the joy in my journey.

So what do I say to people who have known persecution, pain, and great personal loss? I still do not know. But I think I am learning to listen and know that I do not have to have the answers.

An Unlikely Place to Meet a Sister

I met Jesmin on a fast-moving bus hurtling through northeastern Bangladesh. She knew the national hosts we were traveling with.

"I remember you!" she said in her beautiful Bangladeshi-British brogue. Our host had visited her home when Jesmin was a child. As we all got acquainted, she invited us to her home before we left the area of her country. "Come to visit me, and I will prepare a Bangladeshi meal for you. Everyone in the village knows where I live. Just ask for Teacher Jesmin." She was a popular teacher in the school near her home.

We planted the seeds of a friendship there in her home, where we enjoyed her warm hospitality. Jesmin was the person who introduced me to the wonderful world of social media. From there, we moved to a direct messaging platform so that we could have longer conversations. (Those messages were routed to my phone when we were not on the computer at the same time.) Then we moved on to video calls in which we had virtual face-to-face conversations. Since that initial meeting on a bus in Bangladesh, I have visited her in her home twice after she moved. Our friendship continued to grow, and I expect it to continue to do so for a lifetime. I am amazed. You never know when you will find a new friend or a new sister. For us, it was on a bus in Bangladesh. In what unlikely or unseen places have you made a lifelong brother or sister?

A Kangaroo Teaches Me Unexpected Life Lessons

Finally, after seven-and-a-half years of talking about visiting Australia, there we stood. After all, the country is only a few hours' flight from the Central Indonesia island where I had visited twice a year in recent years. In fact, this was my fourteenth visit to Indonesia. The time was right, so we did it. We seized the day. I am so glad we did, since it ended up being my final trip to that part of the world.

I knew when I deboarded the plane and stepped foot on Australian soil, it would complete my visits to all the continents (except Antarctica, which is not on my bucket list). Two She Is Safe colleagues had traveled and served with me in Indonesia the two previous weeks. Our intensive work concerning abuse and slavery prevention and rescue and restoration for women and girls in Sumatra and Central Indonesia was completed for this trip. We looked forward to a few short days of much-needed rest and relaxation before returning home.

We spent the first day hiking to and through a beautiful botanical garden. Then we walked a long way to another location in search of kangaroos—unsuccessfully, mainly because I got another round of a pesky bacterial stomach bug that I could not shake off. But before our departure back to the States, we were determined to locate kangaroos.

After intensive internet research, we agreed on going to a nearby national park that boasted kangaroo sightings. The next morning, we summoned our rideshare driver and were off for an adventure. On our very first step inside the park, we saw a mama kangaroo and her joey. I already felt that my journey was complete. Then, a short walk later, we saw more very close by. It was so exciting! I could not wait to capture the moment on video. We would watch them jump around and do what only kangaroos can do. I could anticipate showing the video to my two animal-loving granddaughters.

I positioned myself and my trusty smartphone and prepared to grab a remarkable video. The kangaroo was supposed to hop around. He was poised to jump . . . and then he plopped over for a mid-morning nap in the sun.

It was unexpected, somewhat disappointing, but mostly funny. When I arrived home and showed the video to my four-year-old and one and a half-year-old granddaughters, they laughed and laughed and wanted to watch it again and again as they held their souvenir kangaroo toys I brought to them.

Later, as I thought about that kangaroo moment, it seemed to summarize my last trip to Indonesia. It also had some unexpected outcomes that brought about a new twist to my mission life story. I know that sometimes, life takes an unexpected twist and turn; and sometimes, it is hard and painful. But it is also absolutely the right thing that brings unexpected peace—just like a kangaroo deciding to take a nap on a sunny Australian morning.

La Reina

That is me—*La Reina*. It is the Spanish word for "the queen." There I was again in the shotgun seat of the fifteen-passenger van, lumbering across the streets of Guanajuato, Mexico. I was leading a mission team of students and adults from our church to do a children's outreach program for five days. Our in-country partner asked me to sit in the front, so we could discuss strategy for the week as we drove back to our hotel. So I did because I was "in charge."

I never really wanted to be in charge. It is not in my nature. I have always felt I was a better follower than a leader. But at that time, I was the mission minister at my church; and part of my job was to organize and lead mission teams. I thought it was a great idea to intentionally involve people in missions both locally and globally. It was, and someone had to be the leader.

There I was again, whether I liked it or not, sitting in the front. My husband thought the nickname he gave me was funny—"the Queen." What is funny is that he still calls me that many years later at home when I am being bossy or insisting on getting my way.

We like to be beautiful. We like to be young and powerful. And we want the world to know it, so we take a picture of ourselves and post it on social media. We are *La Reina*.

When my oldest granddaughter, Leah, was five years old, she liked all the fairytale princesses. There is nothing wrong with that when you are five and the world *does* revolve around you.

The thing is, the world does not revolve around me. I know this. My back porch is my kingdom where I meet God each morning. It is where I come and enjoy the world that God created. And it does not make me feel powerful. Rather, I feel just the opposite. I feel awed, humbled, and small next to His creation. So every time I hear my husband call me *La Reina*, or when I feel the need to post a selfie again, or when I watch another princess movie with Leah, I want to remember Who is in charge of everything. And it is not me.

You Are So . . .

My mission team had just made a harrowing drive from northeast Bangladesh up into India. I had no idea that the foothills of the Himalayan

Mountains touched northern India. It was at that point in my life that I understood the disorientation and dizziness of motion sickness. I needed to stop soon and walk around a bit. This looked nothing like the India I had seen in photos. It was cool, not sweltering hot, and it had been raining. It was not as crowded as I expected.

This was my first visit to India. I would come many years later to the India I had imagined when I went to a city in the southern part of the country. That is where I sat in traffic at the intersection where five congested streets came together, and everybody—I mean everybody—was blowing their horns. There was blaring music and bright colors everywhere—from women's saris to food vendor canopies. It stirred all my senses at once not knowing which one to attend to first—the sweltering heat, the noise from the street, the smell of the engine exhaust, or the swirling, unknown words encompassing me. It was too much. I closed my eyes and imagined the quietness of my home.

That is another story. Northern India was not that for me. We stopped for a bathroom break and stretched our legs. It was just in time for me to take some deep breaths and keep my motion sickness to myself.

As we made our way to the bathrooms, we stepped on stones through a beautiful garden. There were flowers, a variety of crops, and a woman squatting by plants working in the garden. When she saw us, she saw three Western women in our Bangladeshi clothing (a long top, baggy pants, and a scarf) and one Western man with bright red hair. I am sure we were quite the sight.

The woman looked up at us and made eye contact with me. She spoke slowly, trying to find the English words to express herself. "You ... are ... so ... " I smiled and waited for her to finish the sentence. *I am so what?* I wondered. *So big, so amusing, so amazing?*

"You are so ... white!" she finished with smiling eyes.

"Uh ... Thank you?"

She was right. I was so white compared to the dazzling colors all around me, compared to the brilliant beauty that she was. Her skin tone was such a rich, creamy brown. I discovered later in my cultural studies that many people in Asian countries admired the white skin of Westerners. Their dark skin tones meant that they were laborers that had to work long hours in the sun. They were low in their societal structure. If they had lighter skin, that meant they could stay indoors and have someone else serve them.

Is that not ironic? In the States, we pay much money to have our skin bronzed or pay for expensive vacations to sit out in the sun on a beach somewhere. We come back home with skin darkened by the sun. It seems we are never satisfied with how God made us. God, in His wisdom, made us both to reflect Him in all colors.

9
Listen to Unheard Women

IMAGINE SITTING ON THE FLOOR in a humble home of a woman in rural Sumatra, Indonesia. You sit barefooted in a circle of women from the village and enjoy their hospitality. Many of the women have stopped working in the coffee fields to come and join the meeting. They love their self-help learning and lending groups. She Is Safe named them Transformation Groups. Women learn together how to start and maintain small businesses to earn an income for their families. But the real transformation comes in how they have taken steps of faith to life in Christ. Listen as they tell their own stories.

A Life-change Story[15]

My name is Merpatie. I am the bookkeeper for my Transformation Group. I come to this TG to help me in many ways, but it helps my whole family. I want to earn money so I can help my children have a better education. They need to do better than me. Maybe they can even go to university. And I teach them to save money also.

In our TG, when we have problems, we discuss them together and work to solve them together. Such as, problems with husbands, we discuss those problems and find solutions together. Some of the husbands don't want their wives to come to TG and leave their work in the fields. But I am happy because my husband encourages me to come. He notices what I have done

---

15 DeAnna Sanders, "A Prayer Letter from DeAnna Sanders," *Transformation: Indonesia*, May 2013.

to help our sons. He even helps me with the accounting. He is proud of me and makes me feel special. I know I can do many things now and God can do the impossible.

The Power of Change

In March of 2012, two She Is Safe staff members and I traveled to Indonesia. We attended a Transformation Group, where we met Rina and her seventeen-year-old pregnant daughter, Maua. Rina told us of how her husband often physically abused her because of his constant drunkenness. Maua then shared how her husband physically abused her, also, and asked for prayer for him and for her baby to be safe.

Recently, I sat in Maua's home; and as she held her healthy baby boy, Joy, she told me, "Last year, I was pregnant; and I asked the women from She Is Safe to pray for me. They said that prayer is powerful, and it can help you. My baby boy was born healthy, and I named him Joy. Please pray that Joy will become a man of God.

"My husband got sick with an infection and had an operation. I feel the power of God in me in this Transformation Group, and I feel my bitterness for my husband going. Last year, I hated him because he would beat me; and then he got sick. I know the Holy Spirit in me tells me to love him and take care of him. I can't do it, so I know it is the power of the Spirit within me. Please pray that I can be a good wife and love him."

A Poem of Transformation and Inspiration

"I am Mama of Rachel." It was late May in a village in Sumatra, and I was sitting on the floor in the home of Maua, who was holding her baby boy, Joy. Indonesian women introduce themselves as the mother of their firstborn. "I have dua *anak-anak* (two children) and soon satu cucu" (one grandchild, pronounced "choo-choo").

This Transformation Group had already heard about my granddaughter to be born later that year, and they had a gift for me—a selendang sling, a beautiful piece of fabric that twists and ties around the mama into a functional baby carrier. We sat on the floor in a big circle and enjoyed their food and flavorful Sumatran coffee. They gave me a signed photo of the group; and to express her gratitude for our groups coming through the years, the sweet woman stood and read her poem.

I Wonder Why
A Poem of Transformation and Inspiration

Already, I wonder why you call me sister.
But I know you are American, and I am Indonesian.
You are from a great city, and I am from a simple village—
Too much difference.

You call me "My dear,"
Though you don't know me so much.
You only know my name.
We meet once, and I don't understand your language.
You pray for me, even though I only tell you a little.
Neither do I call you.
But why do you love me?

You call me "friend," but you don't know me, my friend.
Even to spell my name is difficult.
It's impossible that I come to your house.
And you don't know my language.
But why do you love me so?

I have become your sister,
But I know actually, I am nobody.
Too much difference.

And now, I know that it's all happened because of Jesus.
Jesus makes us become sisters.
In Jesus, we love each other.
Jesus teaches us to pray for each other.
And the love of Jesus is above all differences.
We love you, my sister.

10
Unseen Precious Children

I COLLECT NATIVITY SETS THAT I have gathered from all over the world—from Mexico to South Africa, from Indonesia to Bolivia. I do not know how many I have—at least twenty or so. I love to bring them out each Christmas season and enjoy how different cultures depict the holy family.

The Nativity that is one of my favorites was handcrafted by my daughter. It is a crocheted set featuring Mary, Joseph, their smiling donkey, and the angel bringing the good news of great joy about the birth of baby Jesus. *Wait!* Where is baby Jesus? Somehow, in all the excitement of Christmas last year, crocheted baby Jesus got lost.

Sadly, in the busyness of our holiday music programs, parties, gift-giving, decorations, Christmas trees, and lights, sometimes, the point of Christmas—the baby Jesus—gets lost.

My daughter photographed a moment when my three-year-old granddaughter, Leah, gathered all the Nativity characters, along with all her toy ponies and cartoon characters. These were some of her favorite and treasured toys. Everyone was invited to join the party. This was an accurate description of my sweet granddaughter: she loved people. She loved her family. And nothing was better for her than when everyone was together. So, naturally, she would invite everyone to join the party and celebrate the birth of Jesus.

The implication was clear. We should all invite Jesus into our celebrations this Christmas. When you are eating your feast and opening your gifts and enjoying your family, invite Jesus to your house and into your heart.

When my daughter read the Nativity story to Leah and explained all about the birth of Jesus, in her excitement, Leah proclaimed, "I want to see Him!" *Me, too, Leah. Me, too.* Seeing the unseen through the eyes of a child changes perspective.

I made a note to ask my daughter to crochet me a new baby Jesus. I want to invite Him to His own birthday party.

I Want to Sit by with You

"I want to sit by with you, Bebe." It was a frequent request from my two-year-old granddaughter, Alex (Alexandra Jane). For her, that meant she wanted to sit on my lap—not by me, not with me, but *on* me.

Her mama tried to explain to her that she could say, "Sit by you," or, "Sit with you." She insisted that it was, "Sit by with you." And of course, my answer was always yes.

I pulled her up onto my lap, and we looked at photos on my phone. Or we colored a page in her coloring book or watched a movie together and had a snack. We just enjoyed the moments together, which were usually pretty short since she was two and had more things to do. When she grabbed her sister's toys, pulled her sister's hair, or spilled her chocolate milk again, I knew that soon, she would flash that sweet smile of hers, bat her big blue eyes, and say again, "I want to sit by with you, Bebe." And, of course, I will pull her up again into my lap.

It made me think how much I do the same with my Heavenly Father. I want to sit with Him. I want to just be with Him, to be together and enjoy the moments, to talk, to listen, and to just be content in being His. I imagine that He would smile when I asked and pull me close to be with Him for a few moments, until I was on to other things because I have a childlike attention span and things to do. He knows I will often ignore Him or not do what He asks me to do. But I will soon return. He will long for the moments when He will hear me say again, "Daddy, I want to sit by with you."

The Language of Children

In all the great places I have been honored to travel to, one of my favorite things to do is observe the children. Now, I am no expert with children. My whole family is great with kids, but I am not. I do not know what to do with them sometimes. Yet, as you have seen, it seemed like many of my mission-related trips have involved taking teams to work with children for Vacation Bible Schools. We played games, ate snacks, and made crafts in Bolivia, Mexico, London, and South Africa. We have played relay games, memorized Scriptures, and prayed with children in Washington, D.C.; Flint, Michigan; Arlington, Texas; and Lake Texoma, Oklahoma. I have observed that children in all of these locations love life—they love to play, eat snacks, and drink red punch. I have heard children sing at the top of their lungs in Spanish, British English, and Afrikaans. I just call it the language of children.

An experience in Bangladesh that is one of the highlights of my encounters involved trying to entertain a small group of children while their parents talked with our missionary hosts. My travel partner, Carolyn, had served a few years in central Mexico. She had learned enough Spanish to be proficient in that country.

As we played with the Bengali children and tried to demonstrate a game for them, we both grew frustrated with the insurmountable language barrier. In a final attempt to get the children to understand, Carolyn started speaking Spanish to them. The children grew quiet and tilted their heads. It was not English. It was not Bengali. What was that string of words?

"Uh, Carolyn, I don't think they understand Spanish, either."

"Well, it was worth a try." We both laughed and got back to playing with the kids. They understood the language of love, which was all we had to offer. And it was enough.

Your One Precious Life

Recently, I have read these words from a variety of sources: "I'm living my one precious life." When I hear something multiple times in a short amount of time (a song, a verse, a quote), I stop and pay attention. It is usually God's way of trying to get my attention. I know; I should hear Him the first time, but my hard-headedness usually blocks out His first few attempts.

At first, I dismissed the words as being trite. I thought, of course, we are *all* living one life. It is all we have. And we *all* are precious. Life is precious. We take it for granted. From abortion to abuse, to being neglected, to indifference, we forget that we *all* are precious; and God gives us all life—a life we should treasure.

"I praise you, for I am fearfully and wonderfully made. Wonderful are your works; my soul knows it very well. My frame was not hidden from you, when I was being made in secret, intricately woven in the depths of the earth. Your eyes saw my unformed substance; in your book were written, every one of them, the days that were formed for me, when as yet there was none of them" (Psalm 139:14-16).

I am reminded of the years I spent in Indonesia as She Is Safe country director. Part of my job was to attend children's outreach events. Those weekly meetings were lively with loud singing, playing games, and hearing Bible stories—and, of course, snacks. But the most important part was that the outreach workers made sure the children heard that they were loved by God. Those words, which we often take for granted in the West, are not always words children in Sumatra hear. I wanted them to hear it, to know it, and for it to shape their lives.

While the children were doing their activities, I would request to talk privately to a few of the girls. I would take time to ask them questions like, "What do you want to be when you grow up?" It never ceased to amaze me that the answers I heard were universal children's answers: "a doctor," "a teacher," "a police officer." The answers varied to my question, "How can I pray for you?" Sometimes, it was, "Help me do better in school." "Help me be a better daughter." "Pray for me because my father hurts me every night."

Before I prayed for them, I said, "Indah, (or *Intan* or *Melati*), please know that you are precious, chosen, loved." I needed them to know it and know that it was true.

We all need to be reminded of this truth from time to time that we are dearly and deeply loved by our Father. He wants us to live our one precious life in a way that honors Him, in a way that reflects Him, and in a way that serves others. For me, that means treasuring my gift of family, of home, and of fulfilling work and guarding my daily time of solitude with Him. How are you living your one precious life? Do you understand that you are precious, chosen, loved?

Where You Are

It was a reality we were all preparing for in the days ahead. My daughter and her family were soon to move to a nearby city. They would then be forty-five minutes away instead of five minutes. My granddaughters—Leah, seven, and Alex, four, at that time—had always lived near us. It was about to be a new day for us all.

One afternoon, a few weeks in advance of their move, Leah and Alex were at our house for a few hours. The girls and I decided to talk a short walk over to the nearby neighborhood book barn. We like to walk and talk and borrow some books to read when we get back to our house. That particular afternoon, I thought I would ask how they were feeling about the upcoming change in their lives. It would mean a change in schools, friends, and the only house they remembered. They would also be further away from their other grandparents (Pa and Mimi) who live in a small town near us.

I decided to put a positive spin on the situation. "What are you looking forward to the most when you move?"

Leah quickly said, "I can't wait to come back and spend the week with Pa and Mimi at their house. That'll be fun."

Alex was still thinking about her answers. So I asked a follow-up question: "What do you like most about being at their house?"

Leah described with great enthusiasm all the fun things at their house—their dogs and games they play.

Finally, Alex answered. "I mostly like it because Pa and Mimi are there." What great wisdom from the mouth of a four-year-old. She just wanted to be where they were.

I have thought about Alex's words and how they applied to my relationship with my Father. As I have maneuvered through the complexities of my recent job change, changes in family, and changes at my church, all of it seemed a bit much on some days. There were days I did not want to work. I did not want to care. I did not want to do anything but drink coffee and sit on my porch. There was nothing wrong with that for a short time.

In the quiet, as I prayed, I heard my Father whisper, "I'm still here. Let's just be together for a while."

Alex had a birthday last week. I wonder what words of wisdom she will have at the ripe, old age of five.

11
A Dog's Perspective on Seeing the Unseen

MEET DR. DAISY, TH.D. (THERAPY Dog). She was a one-and-a half-year-old yellow Labrador retriever and became a certified therapy dog with Therapy Dogs International. Our journey started with therapy dog training when Daisy was invited to visit the four- and five-year-old Vacation Bible School class at church (thanks to the invitation from my good friend, Annette, who taught the class). Daisy loved it. The kids loved her. She seemed to have a gift for bringing joy to people. I think she thought all people were put there for her to love. She loved to greet everyone, and you could not help but smile when she offered her unconditional love. She had something special that I could not ignore. She had a gift to share.

We found a trainer and began the work of teaching her to pass the AKC Canine Good Citizen test and Therapy Dog International test. She passed her tests with flying colors with the help and encouragement of another good friend who worked at the hospital. We had access to medical equipment that Daisy would be exposed to when visiting patients.

Daisy and I went to the hospice center to meet the director and good people of that organization. I was a bit nervous as we drove to our meeting, hoping Daisy would behave and show what a good, sweet dog she was. I prayed as I drove, "God, please help Daisy and me to show Your love and be Your hands and feet—and paws—so others can see You and we can serve You through this ministry."

A few minutes later, Daisy was charming them all. We began volunteering for hospice and visiting sick people who needed a few minutes of petting a dog that perhaps reminded them of their own dogs or their childhood—or maybe just to have a few minutes to forget their pain.

Bringing Comfort and Joy

The journey toward training to be a therapy dog had progressed steadily, one paw at a time for Daisy.

We wondered if part of the preparation process for her had something to do with her months of recovery from hip dysplasia surgery as a puppy. As an eight-month-old puppy, we discovered she had problems with her hips. After surgery, she had to be confined for about four months. Once she began to feel better, she still could only go outside on a leash—no running, climbing, jumping, or even going up and down stairs. Everything a Lab puppy wanted to do, she could not. She learned to stay inside with us or stay in the utility room when we were gone. We wondered if during this time, she learned even more patience, how to handle pain, and how to be more sensitive.

Regardless of how that experience affected her, it definitely made us bond even closer together. After she recovered, grew back her hair, and was able to be around more people, she demonstrated her love for people, especially preschoolers at Vacation Bible School.

Daisy took a big step toward beginning her therapy dog practice by visiting personnel at the hospital. Needless to say, Daisy was a big hit with the directors, as well as other volunteers and even people coming through the lobby while we were there. The funniest part was Daisy's fascination with the revolving door. She just could not understand how that worked but did not hesitate to walk through it a few times.

It was fun to watch how people responded to me differently when I had her with me. They immediately noticed her, softened their expressions, talked to her, and petted her. It was amazing how a dog brought out the kid in adults and made them stop and share a moment with her. I was already beginning to see how a therapy dog brought comfort, joy, and a break from the pains of life.

When the training and paperwork were completed (except for more hospital volunteer training later on), it was time for the real work to begin. I was ready to see how Daisy would provide her own unique method of emotional healing. Sometimes, healing was not part of the picture. Sometimes, death came instead of healing, as was the case for hospice patients. It was amazing how God prepared me for that journey. I had just completed reading two books about death and dying, and I was doing hospice volunteer training. I was not sure why at that point in my life, I needed to learn about death and grief; but God always has His reasons.

Making Friends

I was driving Miss Daisy again—or, I should say, driving *Dr.* Daisy—to another appointment. We were invited again to visit residents at a nearby nursing facility.

As we drove, I turned down the radio; and as is our habit now, I voiced a prayer for us. "Thank You, Jesus, for another opportunity for Daisy to visit with people in need of a special visit today. Please help Daisy be a good girl and for us to make the best use of our time and to be well-behaved guests, so we will be invited back for another future visit. And please, dear God, help us to be Your hands and feet and paws in action so that others may see You through our time there today. Amen."

As we entered the front door, we were personally greeted with a loud, "It's Daisy! Hi, Daisy!" One of the residents remembered Daisy's name from our last visit and warmly welcomed us to her home. Daisy moved up close to her and welcomed the attention and a friendly ear rub.

Immediately, Daisy's training and instincts were tested. She spotted a half-eaten cracker on the floor, and she really, really wanted it.

"Leave it, Daisy," I commanded with my strict mama voice. She remembered her training of not taking food that was not offered to her. But she really, really wanted it. Yet she was reluctantly obedient. Thankfully, a worker removed the temptation, and Daisy could concentrate on her work.

The nursing home director led us into the front room, where about six residents were watching television. Well, some of them were watching television. Most of them were sleeping or staring at us as we walked about the room. The director asked one frowning man if he liked dogs and if he wanted to pet Daisy.

"She's just a big, ol' dog," he grumped loudly. "Why would I want to pet her? Nothing special. Just an ol' dog."

The director calmly responded, "But she *is* a special dog. She's here just to see you."

He responded with a grunt and folded his arms.

The time came to go down the first hall and visit each room that welcomed us in—some residents in beds asleep, others in wheelchairs sitting with guests in their rooms, and even one room with several people doing physical therapy exercises. Daisy gladly walked into each room and nuzzled up to those who welcomed her. Sometimes, if we lingered a few moments too long, Daisy plopped on the floor and made herself comfortable.

"Let's go, Lazy Daisy," I commanded. And she jumped up, ready for another walk down the hall.

As we walked back toward the main room, there was Mr. Grumpy, looking around the corner to see where Daisy was. "There you are again," he said. "Ol' dog."

We walked past him and onto the next hallway. That is where Daisy met a new friend. The young adult girl in a red warm-up suit had Down Syndrome. The girl leaned over, and Daisy got as close as she could. Somehow, Daisy knew this girl was special, and Daisy stayed still a few extra moments longer. The girl kept stretching out her fingers to reach Daisy's head, and Daisy let her. When it was time to move on, the sweet girl was still reaching out for the big, yellow dog. I think Daisy would have stayed longer with her new friend if the director was not leading us on down the hall to visit more people waiting their turn to see their furry guest.

We turned around, and there was Mr. Grumpy again. This time, he smiled at Daisy and then at me. He never said anything but, "There's that ol' dog," but his curiosity and the softened expression on his face revealed that we had made another friend.

A few more visits in rooms and it was time to go. We were invited back next month, and I knew Daisy would be happy to come—especially if the sweet girl in the red jumpsuit was there to rub her ears. She would be happy to spend time with her new friends.

Dog Days

It was Thursday again. That was the day Daisy and I got ready to visit patients and staff at our local hospital. I put on my light blue volunteer vest and clipped on my badge. Daisy saw me get out her vest, and she trotted to the door. She instinctively knew it was time to go.

She jumped into the back of my SUV and squeezed her ninety pounds onto the backseat floorboard. We said our prayer. "Dear Lord, Thank You for my Daisy. Thank You for this opportunity to visit people today. Help us to have listening ears and tender hearts. Help them to see You in us. Thank You, Lord. Amen."

I knew as we drove across town toward the hospital that we were going there to do a good thing. But I had to admit, on that day, I did not want to go. It was exhausting to listen to people and to get Daisy in the right positions and know what to say to patients and family. I was too tired to do this again. I did not want to take a couple of hours and walk around the hospital with my dog when I really wanted to just stay home and rest and get some other work done. But we had promised we would come every Thursday afternoon at 1:30 p.m. as often as we could. So here we went again.

Daisy happily greeted her friends at the front desk and in the financial office. They always gave good ear rubs and, sometimes, even treats. This was one of those days. Daisy was a happy girl. She would have been content to go home after just those few visits. But it was time to board the elevator and visit patients on the upper floors.

After a few brief visits in the hallway with nurses and family members of patients, we turned the corner to a room. Immediately, a young woman saw Daisy and rushed out to talk with us. She dropped to her knees and gave Daisy a huge hug.

"How did you know?" she asked Daisy. "How did you know I needed you today? I love dogs, and I needed you right now. How did you know?" The young lady looked at Daisy's ID badge and looked up at me. "Thank you for bringing Daisy. I needed some therapy."

I looked into the darkened room, where a woman lay sleeping and a man sat holding her hand. "Your family is having a hard day?" I asked.

Still hugging Daisy, the young lady said, "It's my mom. She's dying. The doctor thinks this may be her last day. We love dogs. My mom loves dogs. It's like Daisy knew to come here today. I can't thank you enough for bringing her. She has such sweet eyes. What a good girl."

After a few minutes, we walked on to other rooms to hear other stories and see photos of other people's dogs. I could not get the young woman and her mother who lay dying off my mind. We could not take her pain away. But somehow, hugging a big, lovable yellow Lab with sweet eyes made her pain more bearable for a few minutes. It is those moments that I will remember the next Thursday when it is time to put on our blue volunteer vests and drive across town, again, and pray.

From Ugly Dog to Wonder Dog

She was not a beautiful dog. Ang was ugly by most standards. She was short and squatty with wiry black hair. Her right eye protruded, and she had scars from innumerable flea and tick bites and scars from being beaten by her previous owner. Ang wandered away from her cruel master and found herself homeless, sick, and pregnant—an outcast.

It was the story I had heard all week. But the stories I had heard were about women and children, not a dog. On my trip to Indonesia, while on the island of Sumatra, I heard the unimaginable story of Vera*, a fourteen-year-old girl who had been viciously raped not just once but four times on the same day by her own uncle. After the last vile act, she was found traumatized and bleeding, left alone in a coffee bean field to die, an outcast.

Thankfully, our She Is Safe partners received information about Vera from the attending doctor who cared for her following the series of rapes. The doctor was a believer in Jesus, his kindness and compassion combined with his medical skill to bring healing and hope. The youth leader from our partner organization then stepped into the situation and continued providing love, comfort, counseling, and friendship.

A week later, on an island of Central Indonesia, I found myself, along with others from the She Is Safe group and our ministry partners, sitting in a smoky, stale, beer-soaked, music-blaring karaoke bar. We looked into the eyes of a prostitute. From outward appearance, in her short, tight, revealing red dress, high heels, and thick makeup, Inca* looked like what you would think any prostitute looked like. But when you looked deeper, you saw a mother of two young children who depended on her. Her parents also depended on Inca to provide food and shelter for them. But Inca wanted out. Through teary eyes, she asked us to pray that she could find another job. It was hard to leave her knowing what she would be doing when we left, knowing that we did not yet have answers for her and that God wanted better for her, too. We wanted her to know that there was hope for a better life for her and her family. We did leave Inca, sad, alone, beer-stained, and dirty, an outcast.

Indonesia is largely populated by Muslims, many of whom consider dogs to be unclean. When a young Muslim woman found herself living at the women's shelter operated by one of our She Is Safe partners, she met Ang, the ugly dog. The young woman was a victim of abuse and needed a place to stay to rest and heal before finding a new life. At first, the Islamic woman wanted nothing to do with the ugly, deformed, flea-infested dog. Rema*, director of the women's shelter, told the woman she did not have to be near the dog. Now it was no problem. As the weeks went by, the woman noticed that the previously homeless dog had made herself a new home. Ang had been graciously received and welcomed to the woman's shelter. She had been cared for—bathed and fed and loved. She was no longer an outcast. The Muslim woman soon found herself feeding the dog; and through the days together, they forged a very unlikely relationship. They found a family.

Rema told her, "See, you once didn't have a family, and now you do with us. You have had a hard time in the past, and now you have a hope and a future. You are precious—always precious to us and to God."

There is always hope. Ang had two puppies, and all made their home at the shelter.

Of Pigs, Rats, and an Angry Dog

I loved my job as She Is Safe country director for Indonesia, especially the days when I could sit with women on the floor in their homes and hear their stories, laugh with them, and pray with them. When I did that in a rural village in Sumatra, I asked a lot of questions:

- What do you love about being a mother?
- What has been your favorite Bible story you have shared recently?
- What health lessons have you learned?

There were other questions. I waited for translations and scribbled notes. When I asked the last question, a very animated woman with a big smile offered her response. The circle of women erupted with laughter. I could not wait for the interpretation.

She said, "I learned from our health article the benefits of eating papaya. All my life, I've just been throwing it to the pigs. Now, I know they have been healthier than me!"

Sweet, happy women enjoyed sharing life together in their Transformation Groups. Whether it was learning about the health benefits of eating local home-grown fruit, learning how to make hand soap and selling it, or demonstrating love and patience to their husbands and children, their lives truly were being transformed week by week.

On a different island, one known for its beautiful beaches packed with tourists, I had a totally different experience. Instead of dipping my toes in the warm turquoise waters, I was walking in the dark along an unseen dirt road in a part of the city where most of the entertainment industry's night workers lived in row after row of boarding houses. We were there to visit a young woman and her family I had previously met. I wanted to hear the latest on how she was making a difference and being a light in this dark part of the city.

As we walked down the road to her tiny home, I felt something scamper across my sandaled foot. "What was that?!" I asked my host and fellow co-worker.

He said with a smile, "That was a mouse."

I immediately thought, *That was no mouse. That was a rat—a big one.*

Before I could process that experience, we met with our new friends. Harta* and her husband operated a small restaurant on the side of a busy road. We sat down to eat a meal of grilled fish and steamed veggies. Harta had also opened a beauty salon. She had formerly worked in the largest nightclub and brothel on this popular destination island; and her husband worked as a trafficker, luring girls away from their homes on other islands to work in the nightclub. They had met our co-workers, developed a relationship with them, and, after several months, decided to make life-changing decisions.

I wanted to encourage Harta and pray with her. We also met a friend she had met at the nightclub. This new friend had a complicated faith background. Yet this new friend also began making changes in her life that started her and her family on a remarkably new journey. It was amazing. We sat on the floor of her tiny room in the boarding house and fellowshipped together. My co-workers led a Bible study in Psalms and prayed with them. She was still struggling with the decision to change her life. I felt confident, as she made steps toward understanding, that she would soon join Harta in making this radical life-changing decision. I came to give a blessing to them and left so much more blessed than I could imagine.

On the way back to the car, walking once again on dark, unlit streets, an angry dog locked behind an iron gate let out a blood-curdling yelp. My co-worker, startled by the growl of the dog, jumped and screamed.

I said, "See, the dog is angry at you for your past life."

She smiled and said to me, "Mom, I told you, I don't eat dog anymore."

She was from an island known for their habit of eating dogs, cats, rats, bats—almost anything. She knew that I owned dogs and was a dog-lover. All week long, I told her I was watching her, afraid of her habit of dog-eating.

She always replied, "Mom, I don't eat dog anymore." Sometimes, she added with a smile, "But they were delicious!"

It was a trip to remember, for sure. When I eat papaya, see a mouse, or pet my dog, I remember my recent days in a country of unseen laughing women, a family shining their light, and friends who were making a difference.

* Names changed to protect identity

12

Sharing the Stories of Unseen People

SOMETIMES, I FEEL LIKE I am still moving. I have felt like that most of my life. My family moved a lot when I was growing up. That is the fate of many preacher's families. By the time I was eighteen, I had lived in three states, moved fourteen times, and attended nine different schools. The four years I spent at Ouachita Baptist University felt like I had finally found a home. Four years seemed like such a long time to be in one place.

Johnny and I married in 1983. In that long amount of time, we have lived in only two states, two cities, and four apartments or houses. Growing deep roots and nurturing stability felt so right. It is all my children ever knew as they grew up.

Yet it seemed I needed to keep moving—but this time, in the form of travel, not changing addresses. After much traveling in the States, I got my first passport and stamp to Bolivia, South America, in 2000. Since then, I have traveled internationally at least thirty times to nine different countries. Most of those trips were for my work as my church's missions minister or to Indonesia for She Is Safe. And then, abruptly, it stopped. All of it just stopped. The focus of my job changed, and I put away my passport.

Yet somehow, I feel like I am still moving, like the rhythmic rocking motion of a boat, or the forward hum of your car with lights flashing by. My body and mind have not yet seemed to grow land legs. It is hard to imagine I will not experience that motion anymore. Although my job had the word "global" in it (Global Communications Officer), it required very little travel. I was not in a boat in the dark in Indonesia. I was now in my chair in my office with my laptop. I will not miss the endless trans-Atlantic (or Pacific, or both) flights, hours in a car winding up and down Sumatran mountains or narrow touristy streets of Central Indonesia, the occasional speed boat rides complete with nausea, a mouth-full of the Indian Ocean, or a spinning head. I am sure that God thought it was great fun for eighteen years to put an introverted, claustrophobic homebody on an airplane every few months, packed with people, hurling through the air to the other side of the world.

Then He stopped all that motion for me and allowed me to be home again and to be still. I was grateful to have gone and grateful to be home. I knew my call to go into all the world and share the love of Christ had not changed, just my location. And I was grateful my computer desk chair was in its full and upright position and not equipped with a seat belt.

How Was Your Trip?

"So how was your trip?"

It was a question I had heard multiple times when I returned from my frequent trips to Indonesia. I knew they wanted to hear answers like, "It was great! It went really well! Thanks for asking. I'd love to tell you more about it." I knew they wanted to know that I was fine and that I returned home safely. But I wanted to tell them more.

Sometimes, people would listen to a five-minute answer, and I told them a quick story about some women that were learning new job skills in their Transformation Group and how it was changing their lives. For example, Rosma* was making liquid soap with her group and selling it in the market. It helped her pay school fees for her children to attend school. I could share the story about Rema*, a twelve-year-old girl who had been trapped in sex trafficking but had recently been rescued. She was recovering and doing well in our partner ministry's safe house. She was learning how to trust again, both people and God.

Occasionally, others wanted the twenty-minute version; and other times, church groups or small groups would invite me to hear more of my stories. It was then I shared the story of the young mother, a commercial sex worker, and her husband who worked in a nightclub on a popular Indonesian island as a trafficking recruiter. It was his job to lure young girls into being night workers. They met our ministry partners who lived life differently. Over time, this couple experienced a dramatic life change that impacted their entire family. They walked away from their lucrative jobs at the nightclub and opened a small restaurant. They were not making close to the amount of money as before, but as I sat in their restaurant and watched the smiles on their faces, I sensed their peace and was encouraged that amazing life transformations were indeed happening. I recalled the instances in Scripture that said a person believed, and so did their entire household (Acts 16:31-34). I was personally experiencing modern-day New Testament miracles while sitting on the floor of the small restaurant eating their spicy fish.

I was grateful for every opportunity to share about the incredible brave women and girls I had met and the amazing national leaders we were privileged to work with, who faced obstacles every day that would make the normal person want to quit and run screaming from our churches.

Sometimes, I wanted to say, "This trip was hard, really hard. I was sick some of the time I was there. The travel was difficult, and I am having a hard time getting over this awful jet lag."

That was what I wanted to say the first few days when I was home. But of course, I did not. I hibernated at home and attempted to process the previous two weeks—the people I met, the boats I sailed on, and the incredibly difficult situations in which I met women and girls. It took time to understand why suffering like theirs happened and why precious little girls received such horrible treatment from people they should have trusted.

It took time for me to wake up long enough to know from experience that the overwhelming fatigue would pass in time. I knew that I would catch up on all the work I had to do at home that had piled up for the past sixteen days. I knew that I would take time to pray and let God heal my tired body—mentally, physically, and spiritually. And then, after a few weeks of rest, I would know that in six months, I would pack my bags and journey again to the country and to the people who continued to capture my heart.

Then I would be ready again to answer the question, "How was your trip?" I would smile and say, "It was amazing. Thank you for asking and for praying. It's good to be home. But let me tell you more."

No Place Like It

I remember multiple times while traveling globally that I dreamed of home. I have loved to venture into the great unknown; but sometimes, my travels were not exactly glamorous. There were occasions when I had constant upset stomach, or I missed my family, or I longed for my comfy bed in the middle of a sleepless night suffering from jetlag, or I wanted water I could drink from the tap, or—when I really needed a trustworthy toilet—I wished I could click my heels or twitch my nose and my troubles would be over in an instant. That was not possible, though.

I would not trade my years of traveling for any of the creature comforts mentioned, but I do love my home. I love the familiarity of it. I love the sound of my two Labradors snoozing on my office floor, the cardinals chirping on my deck, and the warm fragrance of my pumpkin apple candles burning on the shelf. There is no place like it.

At my church, we had been reading through the Bible and had just finished 2 Chronicles. Neither I nor anyone in my discipleship group shed a tear when that book was completed. However, I did find a few treasures in these Scriptures I would not have seen before if I had not taken a slow read through those chapters. One phrase especially leaped out to me: "Then the priests and the Levites arose and blessed the people, and their voice was heard, and their prayer came to his holy habitation in heaven" (2 Chron. 30:27). That is so beautiful, so lyrical, so profound.

Indeed, as comfy as it is in my chocolate brown rocker/recliner in my office or kicking back in my beautiful, cozy rocking chair on my deck while sipping my cold brew latte, it would be silly to compare those relaxing home locations to the indescribable holy habitation in Heaven that awaits me. This truly is not my permanent home.

In the small group Sunday morning class that I lead at my church, we were focusing on the heroes of the faith in Hebrews 11. After discussing several people of great faith, such as Abraham and Sarah, the writer of Hebrews explains in verses thirteen through sixteen that they died in faith, longing for a better country. The people he describes were nomads, foreigners, travelers seeking a home. They were without a soft pillow and all the things that would make them feel at home. They were always seeking.

The point is that so are we. As believers in Jesus, we know we live in a world that will not be our forever home. While we are thankful for the abundance He has blessed us with now, we know there is more. There is a holy habitation in Heaven, where we get to be with Him always and with all the people in our lives who are already there enjoying Him. What a day that will be! There is absolutely no place like home. Hope to see you there.

*Names changed to protect identity

Conclusion

HAVE YOU ENJOYED OUR WALKS through my neighborhood? Have you taken some walks in yours? Have you gotten to know anyone as you have walked and prayed? Are there any people you have not seen before? What are their names? We have been to many places on these pages and seen many people previously unseen.

It has been an honor to share my journey with you. I hope it has inspired, encouraged, and challenged you to go where God sends you to the unseen people He wants you to serve. Let me leave you with a few highlights from where we have been through these chapters. I have been learning to see unseen people my whole life.

As a six-year-old child in rural northern Alabama, I remember Mama leading the women's missions group in the front room of our parsonage. I remember listening to the stories of how brave missionaries answered the call to go to exotic places, like the thick jungles of the Amazon, to the bustling, teeming cities of India, to the inner, dark reaches of Africa. Mama's group read the prayer calendar of missionaries who had birthdays on the days they met.

As I grew older, those stories stayed nestled in my inner being. I could imagine being one of those people. I wanted to go, meet the people, write stories, and take photos. I wanted to have my name listed once a year in the mission magazine prayer calendar. I said yes to that direction for my life. I moved to Texas to attend seminary to prepare myself mentally and spiritually. I was excited, eager, and called.

Then came a screeching full stop. Life happened. I met and married a young seminary student, who left his engineering career to answer God's call to become a biblical backgrounds professor. *Yes*, I thought! We could go together to all the above-mentioned places. He could teach, and I could write. We could meet the underserved, the unseen, and the under-loved face to face. We could live in their world and see through their eyes.

But life happened again. A sweet baby girl changed everything. Our graduations came and went; and then, before we could take the next step in our careers, life happened yet again. Johnny's dad became gravely ill and passed away.

We found ourselves at a crossroads. Which way do we go? Should we stay nearby Johnny's mom in Oklahoma and help care for her? Which way was God leading? Where were we in the process of answering God's call for our lives? Should we go back to Johnny's professional field? Or should we pastor a church? What would I do with this baby and my call to international missions? Do we move in with Johnny's mom?

Through a series of events, God undeniably opened doors. A want ad appeared in a newspaper for a job in Johnny's specific area of engineering at an oil industry company. Johnny's mom picked up that paper a second time to see the ad that was overlooked at first glance. That led to a job interview, where Johnny was second on the list to be offered the job because the first one turned it down. God provided lots of open doors. We walked through them.

That was when it happened. After a few months in our new location, in our own home with our four-month-old baby, I had time to ask the question, *Where am I?* I knew I was in southwest Oklahoma in a small town. I knew I was a new mom. But when I looked out the window of my home on the safe cul-de-sac, I knew this was not the jungle view I had expected. What was I to do with this urge to go into all the world to share the love of Christ?

So, I started writing—for mission magazines, denominational literature, and even a novel. I sat at my desk and typed on my clunky desktop computer while my babies took their naps. Martin Luther is quoted as saying, "If you want to change the world, pick up your pen and write."[16]

Eventually, I did travel to those places—from the jungles of Bolivia; to the sweltering inner cities of Bangladesh and India; to the mountains of Sumatra, Indonesia, and to the Cape of Good Hope in South Africa. Then I came home to my family, my cozy chair, and my laptop computer.

I eventually realized that my call did not change, even though my location was not what I anticipated. I saw and met people to serve right where I was—people I had never seen before in my town. I found ways to serve in my church. I saw people in their pain. I found writing on my laptop and using the internet meant I could send those words into all the world. I began to see them and how they served from afar. I discovered the truth for the call to missions is about location—serving right where you are. Using God's gifts to change the world is not just about geography; it is about saying yes to the path God opens before you, locally and globally.

Where am I now? Right where God called me to be. Where are you? Where has your journey taken you? What people have you seen lately that you previously overlooked? I hope you are learning their names, being their friend, and sharing light and life with them in your neighborhood and the nations.

---

[16] "50 Martin Luther Quotes on Love and Hope," Gracious Quotes, Accessed December 1, 2021, https://graciousquotes.com/martin-luther.

Travel Map

ON THE TRAVEL MAP BELOW, the locations mentioned in this book are noted with a pin. Do you have a map where you have highlighted where you have traveled? Alternately, do you have one in which you highlight where you would like to go and check them off as you go? A blank map and other FREE resources, including a Study Guide, are available for you to download on my website: www.deannalynnsanders.com.

Bibliography

"50 Martin Luther Quotes on Love and Hope," Gracious Quotes, Accessed December 1, 2021, https://graciousquotes.com/martin-luther.

Burnham, Gracia. *To Fly Again: Surviving the Tailspins of Life.* Carol Stream: Tyndale House Publishers, Inc., 2006.

Elmer, Duane. *Cross Cultural Connections: Stepping Out and Fitting in Around the World.* Downers Grove: InterVarsity Press, 2002.

Frost, Robert. "The Road Less Taken." Poetry Foundation. Accessed February 22, 2022. https://www.poetryfoundation.org/poems/44272/the-road-not-taken.

Goff, Bob. *Love Does: Discover a Secretly Incredible Life in an Ordinary World.* Nashville: Thomas Nelson, 2012.

Keller, Timothy. *Prayer: Experiencing Awe and Intimacy with God.* New York: Penguin Books, 2016.

Lamott, Anne. *Bird by Bird: Some Instructions on Writing and Life.* New York: Anchor Books, 1994.

"Mother Teresa Quotes." Relics World. Accessed December 9, 2022. https://www.relicsworld.com/mother-teresa.

Pittsley, Tammie, Ed.D. *Rising Above the Fog: A Christian's Guide to Habits for Healing Depression.* Independently published, 2018), 1.

Ripken, Nik. *The Insanity of God: A True Story of Faith Resurrected.* Nashville: Broadman and Holman Publishers, 2013.

Sanders, DeAnna. "A Prayer Letter from DeAnna Sanders." *Transformation: Indonesia.* May 2013.

Strom, Kay Marshall and Michele Rickett. *Forgotten Girls: Stories of Hope and Courage.* Lisle: IVP Press, 2014.

Tagore, Rabindranath. "Rabindranath Tagore > Quotes > Quotable Quote." Goodreads. Accessed January 5, 2015. https://www.goodreads.com/quotes/15762-i-slept-and-dreamt-that-life-was-joy-i-awoke.

"Vocation." The Frederick Buechner Center. July 18, 2017. https://www.frederickbuechner.com/quote-of-the-day/2017/7/18/vocation.

Voskamp, Ann. *One Thousand Gifts: A Dare to Live Fully Right Where You Are.* Grand Rapids: Zondervan, 2010.

About the Author

DEANNA SANDERS ANSWERED THE CALL to write in high school and has not stopped many, many years later. She has written blogs, newsletters, and communication pieces for nonprofits. She has served her church as a missions minister and worked in a global nonprofit as Indonesian country director and as director of communications. She has communication degrees from Ouachita Baptist University and Southwestern Baptist Theological Seminary.

DeAnna lives in Duncan, Oklahoma, with her husband, Johnny, and their two fox red Labradors. She loves long walks, relaxing on her deck, sipping flavorful coffee, and savoring one of the several books she enjoys reading at the same time.

DeAnna fills her weekly newsletter, *A Good Word Wednesday*, with bite-sized slices of life from her own experiences and from those she has met around the world.

For more information about DeAnna Lynn Sanders and *Unseen People*, please visit www.deannalynnsanders.com or email her at deannalynnsanders@gmail.com. Or follow her on social media:

www.facebook.com/DeAnnaLSandersauthor
www.instagram.com/deannalsanders
www.twitter.com/DSandersauthor

To subscribe to her weekly newsletter, visit https://dlscommglobal.substack.com.

Ambassador International's mission is to magnify the Lord Jesus Christ and promote His Gospel through the written word.

We believe through the publication of Christian literature, Jesus Christ and His Word will be exalted, believers will be strengthened in their walk with Him, and the lost will be directed to Jesus Christ as the only way of salvation.

For more information about AMBASSADOR INTERNATIONAL please visit:

www.ambassador-international.com
@AmbassadorIntl
www.facebook.com/AmbassadorIntl

Thank you for reading this book!

You make it possible for us to fulfill our mission, and we are grateful for your partnership.

To help further our mission, please consider leaving us a review on your social media, favorite retailer's website, Goodreads or Bookbub, or our website.

More from Ambassador International

Like a chef who seasons the meal in such a way that the distinctive flavors of each element is enhanced, Brian Onken invites readers of *More Than a Clever Story* into an invigorating and fresh taste of what Jesus says in His parables. Reading each parable attentive to Jesus' own words and the context in which these stories are found, you'll hear the voice of the Savior in renewed ways. No longer will you think of His parables as clever stories, but you'll find them to be life-giving words from Jesus.

Every human heart longs to be truly known and deeply loved. Each person has a God-given longing for fulfillment and a sense of belonging that is met only in a relationship with God. But does God really want a relationship with you? Yes, and He demonstrates His desire for that over and over again in Scripture. *Constant Companion* shows readers how to get past feelings of unworthiness, unwillingness, and other distractions and how to listen to God's voice through the practices of meditation, prayer, and Scripture-reading.

Most of us know Who Jesus is and would admit He was a good and kind Teacher while here on earth. But He is so much more than just a good and kind Teacher—He is our Savior and God and worthy of all our worship. Through an in-depth study into the book of Hebrews, Joshua West and Gary Wilkerson take apart each verse, drawing the reader to a closer look at the Man Who lived here on earth for a short time and then became our Sacrifice to save us from our sins and live with us eternally in Heaven with Him. If you are searching for something more from God, dive into this study and drink in the jaw-dropping beauty of our Jesus.

www.ingramcontent.com/pod-product-compliance
Lightning Source LLC
Chambersburg PA
CBHW070659100426
42735CB00039B/2323